A BEARD I

CW01513985

Travels with the Beard
India

By Fiona Roberts

To see the photos, and for information on other books
by the author, please visit
http://www.spanglefish.com/fionaroberts

CHAPTER ONE

"Grab the chicken!" I yelled, and Tod dropped the large rucksack he had been packing and shot out of the conservatory door in truly Olympic sprinter fashion.

The rucksack, unwisely left to its own devices, toppled slowly sideways, sending bars of soap, bottles of hair shampoo and packs of thermal vests skittering across the slippy wooden floor from its open top.

Tod raced into the middle of our lawn and stopped dead.

Looking slowly around, turning full circle, he stopped again. Then, in the absence of anything chicken-like on the lawn, he stared in the conservatory window at me, raising his arms outwards slightly as he did so, in an almost Gallic gesture.

I'd have to have a word with him about that gesture or he'd be shrugging his shoulders as well soon; but I knew what he meant – he couldn't see the chicken. I pointed helpfully towards the large pile of neatly cut, neatly stacked logs leaning against the six foot fence we share with our neighbour Kevin.

Tod looked over at the log pile and instantly spotted the chicken in question standing within beak-reach of the very top of the pile, and therefore within inches of fun over the hedge in the neighbour's garden. Incidentally, have you seen what a chicken's idea of fun can do to your flower beds?

In a matter of seconds Tod had whisked Andrewetta (it's a long story) off the logs and tucked her under his arm. She glared up at him – yes, chickens do have rather a good line in glares – as he carried her back to the middle of the lawn and set her gently down on the grass. She completely ignored him and stalked off without a backward glance. That's Tod off her Christmas card list.

2

We smiled. Andrewetta has character. We would miss her during the two months we planned to be away this time.

In 2009 we had spent five months in Nepal, most of that time in the small, remote village of Salle which is tucked away in a valley high in the Everest Region of the country. We had gone there to teach English as volunteers in the tiny village school, but were completely unprepared for the fact that our encounters with the children and villagers of Salle would leave a lasting impression on our lives. So much so that our outlook on, and approach to life itself would never be the same.

We were smitten – with the uncomplicated, hardworking villagers; with the wonderful, education-loving children who thought nothing of walking through the forested mountains for two hours, six days a week, to reach their school; and with the breathtakingly spectacular scenery of the Everest Region, high in the awesome Himalayas, towards the very roof of the world.

On our return to the UK in 2009 we managed to keep in touch with Kalyani, the young, energetic, village school headmistress with the delightfully quirky sense of humour.

It was a constant source of amazement to me, a veritable dinosaur, that we would dial her mobile phone number, and if the gods were in a good mood and not too busy that day, we would be able to chat with our friend Kalyani, with grandfather, with Kalyani's Mum, and maybe with a water buffalo or two, as they went about their business thousands of miles away, in a remote village high in the Himalayas. How cool is that!

We returned to that village in 2011 and took as many presents for the villagers and children as we could cram into our luggage allowance. It was a memorable, emotional visit, not least because we could see that in many ways 'the writing was on the wall' for the village of Salle.

Vast tracts of the silent old forest that surrounds the village, the forest that muffles your footsteps and breathes

3

down your neck, had been crudely cut down. The ragged ruins of the once green and vibrant trees, the remains of their trunks now split and shattered, reached heavenward towards a perfect blue sky for the help that would never come.

For news of the Great God Money had reached the valley, and now the forests of Nepal are paying the irreversible price of its pursuit. Even one tree trunk sold to the new 'timber barons' brings in a considerable amount of money, money which would otherwise remain out of the reach of the ordinary villager with nothing to sell.

Kalyani had married and left the village of Salle in 2010. When we returned in 2011 she was living partly in her husband's village, and partly in Kathmandu. But her new husband lives and works in Australia, so Kalyani had begun the long process of applying for a Visa to allow her to join him there.

It was probably around the spring of 2012 that Tod and I decided to return to Nepal. By then Kalyani had begun to throw in the occasional,

"When will you come back? The villagers and children are missing you Tod and Fiona!" at the end of our phone calls to her, and to remind us that her Australian Visa surely couldn't take much longer to arrive. When it did she would leave Nepal to begin a new life overseas, and we had already begun to wonder if we would ever see her again.

We started to feel the now familiar pull on our senses as our thoughts turned more and more towards that little village in the Himalayas; we began to catch ourselves wondering how grandfather was getting on with his bees this year; how our cockerel 'Lucky' was faring, and how our friend Molly was doing. Hardly a day went by without one or other of us mentioning something about Nepal, about Salle, about Kalyani.

We missed them, and wanted to see them again.

The decision to extend our trip, to take in other countries this time, sprang from a number of different factors which I will touch on later. Suffice to say that by January 2013 plans for our next adventure were finalised, and we told Kalyani,

"See you in March!"

"Yeeesssss!" she screeched, and we all laughed. We were going to have fun!

So that is why Andrewetta never made it over the hedge into Kevin's garden, and never experienced the chickeny delight of wrecking his pristine flower borders. We had been finishing the packing for our latest trip when we spotted our feathered mountaineer, and nipped her cunning plan in the bud.

This book is the story of our third visit to Nepal, and in particular of our third visit to the village of Salle. It is also the story of, amongst other things, our momentous trip to Bhutan; and an unintentionally rip-roaring, mind boggling race through part of India.

I feel it behoves me to point out the obvious here – and that is that this book is not written as, nor is it meant to be a 'travel guide', and any references in its pages to places of interest reflect only the impact those places made on *us*.

It is simply *our* story, containing *our* experiences and *our* observations! *A Beard in Nepal 3* provides the reader with a glimpse of certain parts of this wonderful world through our eyes, in much the same way as our first two 'Beard' books have done.

CHAPTER TWO

We forget, don't we? The human brain has a crafty mechanism designed to obliterate those most uninspiring memories, those memories you really ***don't*** want to revisit, of things you swore you would never do again, situations you prayed you would never have to face again.

They are swiftly eliminated, eradicated, consigned to the brain's recycle bin. Gone. Exterminated.

Good, eh?

Well, no; not really. In fact, not good at all, because without that memory to tap you on the shoulder, to whisper in your ear....

We realised within minutes of settling into the hotel micro bus outside Kathmandu airport, and setting off towards the tourist area of Thamel, that things there had changed. And not for the better.

Clouds of grimy dust whipped up by the brisk, hot breeze swirled everywhere, over everything and everyone. The grime has a particular, disagreeable smell, and a matching taste that you remember instantly. There is no escape from it; the grime of Kathmandu seems to possess the ability to home in and settle on any area of exposed skin it can find, and to penetrate even the thickest clothing.

You will be scratching, coughing, and rubbing your eyes in no time at all.

The hotel driver greeted us enthusiastically. He remembered us; well, he remembered Tod and his beard, and reached out to give it a quick tug. Ah, the ancient art of beard tugging remains alive and well in Nepal. Tod grinned.

The Kathmandu roads appeared to be in a worse state of repair than on our last visit two years previously, and God knows they'd been bad enough then. We gazed out the bus window at a quite astonishingly chaotic landscape; one that looked as if the whole area had been bombed, and then haphazardly bulldozed, strewing random piles of stones, bricks and garbage everywhere. There seemed to be even more rubbish around than we remembered, and the blue plastic carrier bag is undoubtedly breeding successfully in Kathmandu.

The garbage lay in thick drifts against walls, lined the edges of the road in place of kerbstones, and poured in massive, unsightly ribbons down the banks of the river we drove across - the river that was already clogged with so much rubbish that the small amount of polluted water in it couldn't flow anywhere.

The monsoon rains when they came would move everything downstream, somewhere else; out of sight, out of mind.

We crashed, bumped and crawled along, somehow avoiding the moving mass of humanity, and the occasional meandering cow, that swayed in uneven waves across the route, and skidding past all manner of other vehicles, each equipped with a noisy horn and shouting driver. Shouting forms part of your contract if you are a Nepali driver, and it is the preferred method of communication in most circumstances.

We peered out the windows at the crowds milling around; at the all too many shades of humanity sitting or lying by the side of the road; at sad eyed women with tiny babies wrapped in filthy cloths and held close, their faces covered against the all-pervading grime; at elderly men sitting cross legged or squatting and staring into space, unheeded by the passing hordes, looking for all the world like badly-made statues which, having fallen off some truck or other were now damaged, unwanted, abandoned, never to be recovered.

This wasn't right, we thought, and not for the first time. The wonderful, long suffering people of Nepal deserve better. But as I write Nepal is considered to be the poorest country in Asia, and the evidence for that ranking was appallingly easy to see along the streets of its capital city. Somehow, wherever we looked there seemed to be more people, more rubble, more decay than we remembered, and the chaos that is Kathmandu, the chaos that is always in your face there, simply screamed at us.

By the time we reached the hotel we were in sombre mood, but the sight of the familiar small side street and hotel entrance, and the staff grinning and waving to us soon cheered us up. They made a fuss of us, and Tod's beard was, as usual, much admired. We laughed. It was good to be back.

We cheered up even more when they showed us to a bright and pleasant room; one of the best the hotel could offer.

Aahh; there is nothing quite like lying back and relaxing on a soft and comfortable bed after a very long and tiring journey.

Well, we'd be able to do that when we got back to the UK; in the meantime we'd be fine on the hard, unyielding bed in the hotel. At least we could have a shower; cold water is always so reviving.

We spent the next day wandering around Thamel, the tourist area of Kathmandu, enjoying the warm weather and renewing our acquaintance with various shopkeepers, taxi drivers and rickshaw riders.

Several shops had closed down since we were last there and the premises lay empty. We realised that one or two of those shops had been run by shopkeepers who we had come to know and like very much, and had been looking forward to seeing again. We had brought photos of them with us, taken the last time we had been in Kathmandu, smiling and waving at the camera.

We wondered where they had gone; why they had closed their businesses.

We soon discovered that the worsening economic situation in Nepal over the past couple of years, and in Kathmandu in particular, had forced several businesses to relocate to smaller, cheaper premises, off the tourist track. But 'off the tourist track' inevitably means less footfall in the shops, and as a consequence, less income for the businesses – a vicious circle in fact, and one that was beginning to close in and suffocate those trapped in it.

We tracked down one shopkeeper to a quiet side street quite some distance from the main drag, and sat down to drink tea with him and half a dozen of his friends.

They bemoaned their fate, and the ever worsening fate of their country. They told us that the Nepali parliament was still in uproar, unable to make progress; the many different political parties seemed incapable of working together, thereby making any semblance of governing the country unrealistic. As the politicians argued, the people of Nepal bore the brunt of the worsening financial instability.

And, as on so many previous occasions, a general strike had been called over the next two days,

"What do they hope to achieve by that?" we asked, unsure who had called the strike and why,

"We have no idea," our friend told us sadly, shaking his head. "Maybe something; maybe nothing," and he sighed.

The unremitting struggle to make a living, to simply survive, had taken its toll over the last two years, and our normally jolly, smiling friend had lost his zest for life. A shadow lay over him, and the bright and hopeful sunshine no longer reached him. We felt sad for him.

He hugged us and wished us well as we left; we knew he genuinely meant it. This lovely man could still find it in himself to wish others well despite the host of unfair disadvantages that life in Nepal was throwing at him.

We had sat through several general strikes in the past, unable to travel anywhere, unable to do anything at all; all shops and offices were closed. One shopkeeper who had the temerity to open up had been rewarded by having his shop burned down. Kathmandu ground to a complete, uneasy halt. We expected this strike to be no different.

But to our surprise maybe 25% of shops in the tourist area were open for business as usual the next day, in defiance of the call for a general strike. Why? Because many of the shopkeepers and business people there have had enough, and they considered this enforced loss of one or two days' takings to be a pointless exercise, and one which would only add to their many existing problems.

There is little electricity in Kathmandu, certainly not during the day. On our previous visit in 2011 the noise of generators struggling to provide light to the shops and offices had been a constant background roar, but this time even *they* were all but silent, having fallen victim to the worsening financial situation. The petrol used to run generators and vehicles alike in Kathmandu comes in from India by road, and when it arrives it is expensive. I say 'when it arrives' because every so often one of the petrol tankers crashes off the high, narrow road and down the mountain side....

Lists of electricity 'black out' times are still distributed every month, and the ever resilient residents of Kathmandu simply sigh, and work round them as best they can. And so it goes on and on, with apparently no end in sight.

It seemed also that the water supply situation in the city had not improved, and water is still delivered in tankers once a week. Those without the luxury of a storage tank still have to collect their water from standpipes in the street, usually in the early hours of the morning.

But although some of the shopkeepers and businesses had now made a stand, and defied the call to strike, there was no transport at all across the country. So we were trapped. Our journey up to the village of Salle was therefore put on hold for two days longer than planned.

We were frustrated, irritated by the unforeseen delay. We wanted to be away, up to 'our' village high in the Everest Region, up and out of the Kathmandu Valley smog and grime, up to see Kalyani and our other friends again. After all, that was why we were there.

Kalyani rang us at the hotel, squealing and giggling down the phone in delight,

"You are back! I will see you soon Tod and Fiona!" she said happily. "But I am in my husband's village now and I have to stay here until after my grandmother-in-law's funeral ceremony," she told us, "so I will not be able to travel to Salle with you. But I will meet you there, in the village, and come as soon as I can."

Tod and I looked at each other. We understood the necessity for her to take part in the funeral ceremony, of course we did, but that was not good news for us.

We had several large and heavy rucksacks stuffed with presents for the villagers and children, and would be carrying quite a bit of money with us to give to them too. On our ten, maybe twelve hour journey up to a remote, isolated region of Nepal, not far from Everest Base Camp, and very far from 'civilisation', we would immediately become a potential target for the unscrupulous have-nots, and would almost certainly not reach the village with our rucksacks or money intact.

We knew that. But so did Kalyani,

"You must not go alone," she continued. "It is too dangerous these days. I will send my youngest brother to travel with you."

Problem solved.

Please don't get the idea that Nepal as a whole is dangerous for foreigners; I don't think it is. But you do need to have an awareness of potential problems; only a fool would disregard a warning, anywhere in the world.

Now here's an odd thing:

Nepal is usually five hours ahead of the UK. At least it *has* been, on each of our previous two visits.

But believe it or not some fiendish quirk of fate has provided Nepal with an extra fifteen minutes! Yes! I kid you not! Nepal is now five hours and *fifteen minutes* ahead of the UK.

What on earth has happened? Where have they nicked it from? Has Nepal somehow moved through space faster than us? Have we in the West stumbled and lost a quarter of an hour somewhere along the way? Is our fifteen minutes floating around in the ether discarded, confused and lost? Will an astronomer spot it one day heading in our direction, trying desperately to catch us up?

Or is there someone out there somewhere who should have been famous?

CHAPTER THREE

Hello; do I know you?
Oh yes, yes of course I do. I remember now.
Come in, come in.
Lovely to see you again after so long.
It must be, what, maybe two years?
Yes, you've been a stranger for two years at least.
I'm not sure I remember the name after so long.
What shall I call you?
What? Sorry?
Oh, ok, *'Imodium'* it is then.

We waited around in the hotel, chatting to fellow
travellers, reading the local English language newspapers,
unable to start our journey up to the village because of the
general strike.

The grimy heat of Kathmandu began to get us down.
The polluted air left an unsavoury, gritty taste in the mouth,
and it took only thirty minutes outside for your finger nails
to collect a crust of grime beneath them, gathered simply
from the air.

As time went on our frustration grew and I began to
whinge, something I do really well. Tod ignored me. He
usually does. He's used to it.

The hotel we always stay at has a small, high-walled
garden outside. It is a veritable island of calm in the sea of
chaos that is Kathmandu, with tropical flowers growing in
large terracotta pots, and a slender, elegant tree in the
centre, its leaves casting shade and cool air beneath it.
There are fascinating carvings on the walls of ancient
Buddhist and Hindu stories, and odd, stylised elephants and
tigers depicting the Creation.

"Oh look," I said one evening as we sat outside at a table in the garden, "they've got some new statues over there."

Tod glanced over his shoulder in the direction I indicated, turned back, and said nothing.

I stared at him. He can be strange sometimes,

"Three of them;" I said, "statues; over there. They're new," and I prodded an indignant finger towards the three unfamiliar figures standing at the far side of the garden.

Tod looked at me and shook his head slowly before looking away. But he still said nothing. Have I said he can be strange?

I sighed.

A smiling waiter appeared and we ordered something to eat,

"They're new," I said to the young man as he finished noting down what we wanted. He looked at me quizzically,

"Those statues over there," I said, and I pointed yet again towards the three figures.

Would you believe; the waiter looked over, and then just walked off without a word or a backward glance! How rude.

"Fo?" Tod said quietly, "Have you got your distance glasses with you?"

"No. Why?" I asked,

"Well," he said, "those 'statues' are actually table umbrellas. They're down, you know, not put up; but they *are* umbrellas."

I glared at him. It was obviously a trick of the fading light.

Tod had the good sense not to smile.

I mentioned previously that we were pleased to get a bright, airy room on the second floor at the front of the hotel. It overlooked the narrow side street, and also the hotel's small car park with the large metal gates that were closed and locked every night.

Trucks and delivery vans are not allowed into Kathmandu during the day, but the night brings a veritable, jostling free-for-all as all manner of heavy vehicles rush into the city.

We had noticed that a school a short distance from the hotel had been demolished, and work was going on behind high security fences to lay the foundations for a new shopping area.

Now sleeping peacefully is not something that I necessarily associate with Kathmandu. In order to sleep peacefully one would need a certain amount of, shall we say, peace, and peace is in very short supply indeed in Kathmandu, day or night.

The hotel staff get up at 4am to start their working day. I know that because they all have contracts stating that they must *shout* good morning to each other from wherever they happen to be standing at the time. That may be outside your room, or perhaps at the end of the corridor.

Others have contracts obliging them to drop something heavy every morning and then argue loudly with colleagues over who is going to clear it up.

Because of the heat we slept with the mosquito grills closed, but the windows open to let in what little cool air there was. At midnight on our first day we were rudely awakened by what we both immediately thought was the deep rumbling crash of an earthquake, followed closely by a sound reminiscent of a building being demolished or collapsing.

We shot out of bed and stared out the window, expecting to see buildings crumbling all around us. But no. Nothing. The side street was perfectly quiet and deserted, and the car park was silent. The security guard was sitting by the gates smoking.

Just as we were getting back into bed the sound came again. This time Tod recognised it. It was the sound of a truck dropping off a load of bricks at a building site. Ah; the new shopping area just round the corner. Of course.

The rumbling, crashing sound continued at regular intervals for most of the night, and the next night, and....

Oh dear. I don't manage very well if I don't get my quota of sleep, and of course I have single handedly raised whingeing to the lofty heights of an art form.

I fell over the straps of our heavy rucksacks that were standing by the door of our room, and banged my knee on a chair.

Tod's fault for leaving the rucksacks there.

I dropped the only dry towel on the dusty floor, rendering it unusable at a strategic moment.

Tod's fault again, for some reason or another.

I couldn't find my hairbrush. Tod's fault of course.

And for the piece de resistance I took the top off a tube of face cream, and under pressure from the altitude it shot me neatly in the eye....

Before I could say a word, actually it would probably have been several, Tod said,

"We need to go and spend some time at the Garden of Dreams," and he smiled that smile of his that makes everything ok again.

"Yea!" I said, "Come on, let's go!"

So we went.

We left the hotel and walked slowly and carefully along the narrow, early morning streets of Thamel. We walked past the shops that were just opening up; jumping every so often to avoid the water that most shopkeepers habitually throw down outside their shops to keep the filthy dust at bay, and laughing when one of them deliberately aimed a spray at us.

We swayed nimbly, like old professionals, out of the path of speeding scooters and motorbikes; jumped quickly out of the way of dashing taxis; politely refused rickshaw rides; and laughed as Tod was offered drugs for the umpteenth time,

"Do I *look* as though I smoke it?" he asked, peeved,

"Yes!" I told him, "No doubt about it!" and we laughed again. For it cannot be denied that Tod does indeed resemble an old hippie!

We left the tourist area and began to walk along a wide boulevard. It should have been a beautiful road; it *could* undeniably have been a beautiful road. But it was dirty, filthy; the discarded papers, plastic bags and rubbish had piled up in unsightly drifts along the middle of the road, and all along the gutters. Bizarrely, broken bricks and stones lay in piles here and there on the road and on the pavements, but there was no clue as to how or why they had got there.

The litter catches your attention, pulls your eyes towards it, makes you wish that someone somewhere would clean it up and restore some dignity to a once truly majestic city, and thereby to those who call that city their home. Kathmandu is drowning in garbage.

The boulevard was lined with street sellers standing or sitting on the wide, dusty pavements, holding their goods out to us in the hope that we might want to buy a small statue of a Buddha or a Hindu god, a DVD or a pashmina. Beggars, many of them crippled, many of them children who may or may not have had parents, pleaded for Rupees.

We walked in silence, weighed down with guilt.

A high wall, high enough to block any view of what was behind it, loomed on our left. We walked along beside it and in a minute or two reached a small doorway in the wall. The words 'Garden of Dreams' were carved into the brickwork above the door and we walked through and turned sharp left.

The ticket seller smiled at us and we passed our money through the glassless window and took the proffered tickets.

Half a dozen steps later we entered the Garden of Dreams. We might almost have entered a totally different world.

We stood and stared around, marvelling at the sight that had unfolded in front of us. The noisy rush of jumbled sound from the boulevard outside was suddenly so muted as to be almost completely excluded, and the filthy, grime-filled air that habitually blankets Kathmandu was kept at bay there in the garden by the tall trees and gentle breeze.

We breathed deeply. The unexpected elegant beauty of the scene transfixed us – this is surely a place to visit before you die.

A couple of nosey chipmunks raced across the grass to us, stopping within feet. But they decided we were not worthy of further investigation, dashed off, and raced each other up the thick trunk of an impossibly tall, exotic looking tree nearby. We laughed.

Then we strolled over the wonderfully thick and green grass and up a gentle slope to what looked like a perfect Victorian band stand. We sat down together on the seats that lined the inside, and stared around in peaceful (yes, *peaceful*) silence. We were alone in the garden at that early hour.

The Garden of Dreams is described as a 'neo-classical historical garden' and was created by Field Marshal Kaiser Shumsher Rana in the early 1920s. It was his private garden, designed in Edwardian style by two prominent architects of the time; Kishor Narsingh and Kumar Narsingh Rana. These were the men who had designed the Singha Durbar (Lion Palace) in Kathmandu, which remains today the official seat of government of Nepal.

The Garden of Dreams is dedicated to the six seasons of Nepal:

Spring; early summer; summer monsoon season; early autumn; late autumn; winter, and originally contained six impressive pavilions, each dedicated to one of the seasons.

We gazed around at ancient Greek-style beauty, at the amphitheatre, at European inspired facades, at pergolas, urns and birdhouses, at the most beautiful classic-style pond, all surrounded by high trees, neatly clipped hedges, and attractive flower beds.

After the Field Marshal's death the garden was given to the government of Nepal, but was not maintained, and quickly fell into disrepair, remaining as something of a wilderness for decades, forgotten by the world; a kind of secret garden hidden behind its towering wall.

The recent restoration of the Garden of Dreams was financed by the Austrian Government, and took seven years. It was finally opened to the public in 2006. However only half of the original garden has so far been restored, and just three of the six pavilions. Today it covers 7,042 square metres.

We wandered around, across grassy lawns, up old stone steps, round pools filled with clear water and overweight goldfish. We stared up at the unfamiliar trees that leaned high above us at odd angles, their tufts of large shiny leaves at the very top of their otherwise bare trunks waving gently in the breeze. We gazed at the colourful, unfamiliar flowers with the strangely attractive perfume that wafted over you unexpectedly as you turned a corner.

We sat down under the high, cool columns of one of the pavilions and had coffee, served to us by a friendly, softly spoken waiter. He told us how proud he was to work in the Garden of Dreams. We understood.

Later, when the garden had worked its magic on us, and we felt refreshed and renewed, we left that peaceful, elegant oasis of calm, and walked once more back through the teeming, airless streets of Kathmandu, ready to face the forthcoming journey up to the village of Salle.

CHAPTER FOUR

Kalyani's youngest brother looked twelve years old but was actually seventeen, and studying at a college in Kathmandu.

I'm sure I've mentioned previously that Kalyani holds a place in the World Book of Records for having the greatest number of aunts and uncles. It was a source of constant amazement to us that anyone could have so many. Where on earth did they all come from? She used to giggle at us as we tried to work out who was who, where, and why. Eventually, inevitably, we gave up.

However, extra brothers now seemed to be popping out of the woodwork too. We decided not to ask any questions. Always best.

This particular extra brother came with us in a taxi to the bus station to buy the tickets that would get us up to the village. The bus station is not one of our favourite places. In 2009 it was nothing less than a stinking pit   I did attempt a description of it in our first book.

In 2011 we were pleasantly surprised to see it had been somewhat cleaned up; but alas, this time it seemed to have slipped back into the realms of unbelievable filth, and massive piles of crawling rubbish. We cringed, and tried not to breathe too deeply as we made our way to the ticket office.

The story of our time in Nepal is very much tied in with the stories of our chaotic, fun, and often nail-biting journeys in that country. Each journey is an adventure, and no two journeys are ever the same. Nothing is predictable where travel in Nepal is concerned. We know that.

But when the ticket seller told us that there were no longer any micro buses running on the route we would have to take up to the village, our hearts sank.

That meant we would have to travel in a Local Bus. And that was much more risky to life and limb.

The Everest Region of the country (the clue's in the name) is a region of high, narrow, rough mountain tracks, and of course the safety barrier hasn't yet been invented in Nepal. Only the previous month another Local Bus had slid off the track and down the mountain killing twenty six of its occupants.

But short of renting a car and a madman to drive us, our options were limited. So we went ahead and bought tickets for ourselves and Kalyani's brother, and one for our rucksacks so they could ride with us inside the bus. Leaving them unprotected on the bus roof would have been asking for trouble.

We arranged for the hotel reception to call us at 5am, and Kalyani's brother said he'd knock on our door at 4.45am. The taxi was due to pick us up at 6am. We were finally ready to leave for the village. Yippee!

Now there is certainly something exceedingly odd going on with time in Nepal. Time keeping is not a known Nepali strength and a day late, or a day early here or there is considered acceptable in most cases. But when Kalyani's brother knocked on our door at 4am, and the hotel reception rang us at 4.30am, we *did* do a bit of dark muttering. Well, *I* did.

But ok, we were up. No problem.

We were prepared for the lack of electricity at that time of the morning, and were expecting to have to do a bit of bumbling about in the darkness. But we had our torches ready, so I trotted into the bathroom to wash.

Every bathroom in the hotel has an open vent in the floor, out of which a faint odour of sewers will often creep, filling the room with a disagreeable smell that seems to stick to the towels and sneak invisibly onto your clothes too.

But you get used to it, and it had never bothered us.

21

I settled the torch on the tiled floor avoiding the cracked and broken ones, found toothbrush and toothpaste, and began to brush my teeth carefully, using water from our lifesaving filter bottle, and leaning over the basin.

For a change there was complete silence in the hotel, and the sound of the water running down the drain seemed very loud in the small bathroom.

Suddenly, without warning there was an odd gurgling noise from behind me, and before I could react in any way a huge bubble of putrid air belched out of the vent on the floor and completely enveloped me in the worst, the most abominable, disgusting stink I had ever experienced.

I retched, dropped my toothbrush and the water bottle, ran out of the bathroom and threw up in the bedroom.

Tod grabbed me and sat me down on the edge of the bed, then quickly slammed the bathroom door shut against the raging stink inside. I sat shaking, feeling sorry for myself.

Unfortunately we needed our washing stuff, but it was now held hostage in the bathroom by The Stink.

In situations like these, which I daresay for most people are unsurprisingly few and far between, you need a quick thinking Tod. Never one to let the grass grow beneath his feet he grabbed my perfume, opened the bathroom door, and emptied most of my precious Opium into the stinking haze inside.

Right-oh. My Opium versus The Stink. No contest! The perfume won hands down. Could this possibly be, I wonder, the strangest use of a perfume ever chronicled? Heaven only knows what Mr Yves St Laurent would have thought about it.

Carrying my heavy rucksack downstairs was the usual awkward, tripping, sliding affair it often is for me, and I bumbled through the dark hotel corridors whingeing as I went, eventually arriving panting and ruffled in the hotel lobby. Tod and Kalyani's brother were already there.

We dumped our rucksacks by the hotel front door just as the night porter opened it for us. He smiled and wished us a safe journey, and picking up our rucksacks, *all of them at the same time*, carried them outside onto the hotel steps for us.

I stared hard at him, that short and slender young man, who was as skinny as a whippet on a diet, and wondered how much spinach his mother had fed him as a child. Remarkable stuff, spinach.

Oddly enough the taxi arrived at 5.30am instead of 6am. But hey-ho, at least it arrived!

We had made the thirty minute journey from the hotel to the bus station many times, and I had always been amazed at the numbers of people, animals, cars, bikes and rickshaws that thronged the early morning streets of Kathmandu.

But now barely a car passed us, and hardly a person crossed the road in front of us. Gone was the urgent hustle of tangled humanity, and the crush of pushy cars and jostling bikes that we loved to be part of at that early hour.

Was that a sign of the economic downturn? Where *was* everyone?

Actually, they all seemed to be at the bus station; the place was packed when we arrived there. The taxi dropped us at the front entrance of the wide, open air space that most of our journeys around Nepal had started from, and Tod and I picked up our rucksacks and followed Kalyani's brother in through the gates.

We made our way carefully through tight crowds of people who were milling around, bumping and jostling as they passed each other; stumbling over men, women and children sleeping on the ground, their forms barely seen in the still dim light.

We found our bus. It seemed to have the required number of wheels, so we got on taking our rucksacks with us. We had warned Kalyani's brother that based on past

23

experience we may have trouble about the rucksacks accompanying us on board, and advised him to have their tickets handy.

Good thinking as it turned out, because it only took five minutes for the dozen or so passengers already seated on the bus to begin staring at and complaining about our rucksacks taking up a seat. But right on cue Kalyani's brother stood up, whipped the ticket out of his pocket, and holding it up he waved it about a bit, rather like a New Age Neville Chamberlain,

"Look! Look!" he cried, flourishing the small piece of pink paper, "The rucksacks have their own ticket!"

Around us frowns were rapidly replaced by smiles, and we and our travelling, seated luggage instantly became yesterday's news. Neville sat back down and grinned at us, "No problem!" he said. We smiled.

Dawn had broken, and the gentle early morning sunshine sent shadows bobbing across the hard clay surface of the bus station, and shockingly illuminated a wall of rubbish maybe 25ft long and 3ft high, situated just alongside the bus. So that was where the awful, gut-churning smell that had crept silently on board was coming from.

We were glad when the bus got going and moved away from the sea of rotting material that would probably never be cleaned up.

We set off along the Kathmandu Valley on the first stage of what would be a ten or maybe twelve hour journey, travelling the road we had travelled so often, past the now familiar buildings with patches of bare, rubble strewn land nestled between them. We bumped and crashed along on the rough and broken surface, swerving and braking to avoid now a meditating cow, then a car on the wrong side of the road, all the while trying to keep our bouncing bums in touch with the small, hard seats! We stared eagerly out the bus window, loving every minute of this latest adventure.

We stopped several times along the way to pick up new passengers, and the noise in the bus grew louder and louder as the constant, strident Nepali music from the old cassette player on the dashboard struggled to compete with the laughter and shouted conversations going on all around.

There were about forty seats on this Local Bus, and when they had all been taken new passengers began to stand in the aisle. No self-respecting Nepali bus would travel anywhere with even an inch of spare space in it, so crammed and overflowing aisles are the norm. And matching crammed and overflowing roof space is indeed a sight to behold, as humans, chickens and goats cling on, and sway and bump in unison around bends and over rough tracks.

Of course every space on a Nepali bus is smaller than you'd find on a coach in Europe or the USA. Most of the Nepalese people are considerably smaller than us. But this particular bus seemed somehow *much* smaller than we'd previously experienced, and it was impossible to sit straight with legs out in front. In order to fit we had to slant slightly to the side, with knees pointing left or right. But it wasn't a problem. We were used to a certain amount of squishing there in Nepal.

On this journey Tod was sitting by the window and I was in the seat next to the central aisle.

As we careered nearer to the foothills of the Himalayas the aisle filled up with swaying, seatless travellers, who at each stop were pushed relentlessly further along the bus by those determined would-be passengers who crammed in through the door at the front.

Eventually the human crush could move no further and began instead to overflow across the seats, and across those of us unlucky enough to be sitting in them.

In no time at all I was squashed hard against Tod, and unable even to lean back in my seat because the aisle-dwelling woman, who had some time ago leant forward and rested her head on the top of my seat, had now begun to snore, and her right arm had slipped down behind my back. I hoped she wasn't in the habit of dribbling in her sleep.

Now it must be said that the Nepalese people do not harbour any principles of personal space. Not for them the niceties of a bit of distance. And nowhere is that more suffocatingly obvious than when travelling on a Local Bus.

I couldn't move, could hardly even turn my head, and I began to sweat with the fear of confinement in a small space. The bus was by now massively overcrowded. The row of sandal-clad feet hanging down from above, outside the window, attested to the fact that the roof space was also crammed. I wondered miserably how strong the roof was, and if we'd survive if it caved in on us.

We started to climb up and out of the Kathmandu valley and the bus, its overburdened engine roaring, slowed to a crawl. It laboured up the hills, bumping and crashing into craters, bricks and stones scattered around on the rough surface of the track. My new close friend snored even louder. No one batted an eyelid.

The bus swayed ponderously around narrow bends, leaning over further and further, pulled down by the weight of too many passengers, seeming often just beyond the point of no return, and then somehow crashing, creaking and groaning back onto its wheels in an upright position.

The scenery outside the bus windows changed quite quickly from the smog-laden, jumbled brick factories, half built houses, and pocket handkerchief patches of cultivated land of the Kathmandu Valley, to the steeply sloping, thickly forested lower reaches of the magnificent Himalayas. The air that reached in through the small, open windows of the bus now felt fresher, cleaner, and Tod and I smiled at each other; we were really on our way.

Suddenly a wall of squealing Nepalese men, women and children, rocked by a particularly violent movement of the bus as it negotiated a bend, swayed back and forth in unison in the aisle, clutched at each other, lost their balance and fell on me in a giggling heap.

In complete panic I began pushing them off me, shouting and trying to catch my breath, but it was Tod who grabbed and shoved, leaning across me to push them off and back into the aisle, pulling me as far as he could towards the comparative safety and open air of the window.

I wanted off that bus! I wanted to scream and run for the door! I wanted to get out into the open and be able to breathe freely. But of course that was exactly the problem – I knew I couldn't move *anywhere* – I was trapped. I couldn't even change places with Tod; there was no room. So I just had to try to breathe deeply and cling on to my sanity.

Time passed very slowly, and the journey seemed to take ages. The crowd in the aisle hung on in there and went with the flow, smiling and chatting as if they weren't really being thrown around like corks in a stormy sea. I marvelled, yet again, at the resilience and patience of the Nepalese people.

Ten hours later we reached a town, albeit a very small one by Western standards, and there we stopped.

I'm reasonably sure that the town of Chericote, which we had reached, has a local bye law that obliges its residents to walk up and down the main street and round the square constantly. Because that is just what they do, in colossal, moving waves of noisy, colourful humanity. We watched, fascinated.

Chericote is pleasant. Surrounded by massive, peaceful, snow-capped mountains as far as the eye can see, it has a number of colleges, an international hospital, and a bright and vibrant young population not so very different in outlook and aspiration from any young population in the

West. We stared out the bus window at gossiping groups of denim clad youngsters in brightly coloured t shirts splashed with English language logos; at older men wearing traditional Nepali dress, driving patient water buffalo slowly across the square to who knows where (lovely creatures, water buffalo; the ones that live and work on the terraces around the village of Salle are quite chatty); and at older women, also in traditional dress, sitting in groups at the side of the road watching, like us, the passing spectacle.

How different life in Nepal must seem to them now compared to when they were young. *Change* has positively sprinted into the country, leaving a bewildered, older, traditional generation looking on in disbelief and incomprehension as the younger generations attempt to embrace what it has to offer.

Our bus edged slowly through the happy melee that blocked the road, horn honking and driver shouting, making for a relatively clear space just across the square, in which the bus eventually stopped. A moment's pure undiluted peace sped through the bus as the deep, ragged roar of its engine died away, and took the juddering movement of constant vibration away with it. Our ears breathed deeply and relaxed.

But the moment passed all too soon and was replaced rather shockingly by the commotion created by twenty or thirty passengers who now began getting ready to exit the bus. A similar number had assembled outside the bus door, waiting to get on board and replace those who were leaving. We sat quietly, looking around.

Now here's a strange thing. There is without doubt a Wicked Gnome in Nepal that blinds the travelling Nepalese to the fact that in order to exit a bus the way must be clear and free of *in*coming travellers. And conversely, in order to board a bus the way must have been previously cleared of all those travellers wishing to exit said bus.

But sadly the Wicked Gnome is stronger and craftier than anyone can imagine and keeps Common Sense locked up in a deep, dark cavern, from which it seems unlikely he will ever escape.

Tod and I watched open mouthed as Nepalese travellers *literally* climbed over one another in an attempt to either enter or exit the bus *at the same time!* We are talking old ladies, babies, young men and women, the works! That Wicked Gnome really does have a lot to answer for.

But over and above the inevitable mayhem unleashed down the centre aisle of the bus as a consequence of this simultaneous entry and exit battle, came the sound of laughter and cheery greetings. There was not a frown or angry word anywhere! How cool is that.

Eventually, when some semblance of order had been restored, and the vacated seats were filled once more, we set off again and an hour later reached the small village of Cowah. It was here, at the top of the valley, that we had previously always left the bus in order to walk to Salle, as the only track down the mountain to the village was all but impassable except by the sturdiest of trucks. However, we had been told that it was now possible to reach the village of Lohrimani by bus, and we were curious to see the new track which had been dug out of the mountain side for this very purpose. Lohrimani is just one hour on foot from Salle.

At first glance Cowah did not seem to have changed. It is barely more than a collection of one storey buildings built along both sides of a single, narrow street. If you follow this street out of Cowah for roughly ten miles you will reach Jiri, a small town through which those wishing to climb the mighty Everest must pass, as indeed did Edmund Hillary and Sherpa Tensing in 1953. Jiri was at that time Everest's Base Camp.

We had spent many hours in Cowah during our visits to Nepal, waiting for one bus or another, and had nicknamed it 'The Village of the Damned'. Curiously enough it looked just like the set of an old Hammer House of Horrors film, and I wouldn't have been surprised to see a dark and ominous looking Peter Cushing, or a devilish, be-caped Christopher Lee lurking in the shadows somewhere nearby.

The buildings in Cowah are mostly constructed of wood with roofs of corrugated tin. Conversation would become all but impossible inside the houses when the Himalayan rain hammered down in massive drops on the village, as it often did.

But the reason we had chosen such an unkind nickname for the place was that it appeared to be covered in a thick film of heavy black dust. It was everywhere, lying in uneven layers across the road, and around the houses. It made the village itself seem dark and foreboding, and the villagers appear unwashed and somewhat sinister. Even the chickens that dashed here and there, scratching for seeds and anything else they could find, were grubby, their feathers uncharacteristically unkempt. Did you know that the chickens that live in Cowah are the Linford Christies of the poultry world, and hold the record for the speediest chickens, with the longest legs, anywhere?

Oddly enough we had never discovered the source of the black dust in Cowah, and Kalyani had not known the answer when we asked her about it.

The bus now stopped in the middle of the only street through the village. As the engine's roar died away Tod and I turned and looked expectantly over at Kalyani's brother,

"No, no," he said, understanding our unspoken question, "we don't get out here anymore. The bus goes on to Lohrimani now, so we don't have to walk so far," and he smiled tiredly at us.

We settled back into our seats to wait. It was quiet in the bus; even the constant Nepali music had stopped. A group of local store keepers gathered outside the bus door, and when it swung heavily open with a creaking crash they quickly began loading their wares up the steps and into the bus.

The aisle rapidly filled up with huge sacks of rice, boxes of bottled beer, and large and heavy packages of dress making material. It crossed my mind that there was no particular order to the distribution of this pile of travelling wares, and it grew bigger, wider, and eventually became a three foot high barrier spanning the aisle and extending along half the length of the bus.

When everything was loaded in, and the last of the store keepers had shouted their thanks to the driver, the now all too familiar stuttering rumble of the engine started up again. We were on our way.

However, that Wicked Gnome had a trump card up his sleeve, and he played it now. Astonishingly, half a dozen passengers stood up and shouted to the driver that they wanted to get off.

What? Surely not!

Actually, *probably* not, as the exit was well and truly blocked.

But seemingly undaunted by what stood in their way, those passengers who wanted to get off the bus now proceeded to attempt to do just that.

They scrambled and climbed, they slipped and tripped, they abseiled over seats, they laughed and squealed, and…. they made it to the exit. I wanted to give them a round of applause for their efforts! What a floor show!

Now, you may well be thinking that we then got underway again. Well, you'd be wrong. And that's because another half dozen travellers got on board. *Oh yes they did!* They scrambled and climbed, they slipped and tripped, they abseiled over seats….. Except, that is, for the elderly lady that Tod and I lifted over a stack of rice sacks for, unable to cope with the pressure of many feet climbing on it one of them had split, and had spilled its contents over the floor and nearby seats. Slippy stuff, raw rice. The elderly lady grinned at us and reached out and gently touched Tod's beard. We all laughed.

And then off we went again, driving slowly through the village of Cowah, on the final leg of our journey to Salle. We stared out the window wondering where the new track was, the one which would take us down the valley to Lohrimani. But when the bus eventually turned off the road onto a steep downward track, we were completely unprepared for the route it then took.

CHAPTER FIVE

The bus plunged down the steep track that had been roughly but determinedly gouged out of the mountain side, and for twenty minutes or so slithered along on the dry, startlingly red clay surface at walking pace, allowing us time to take stock.

It was indeed a new track, but the most astonishing thing was that alongside the new track a veritable village of new houses had sprung up on both sides. For the most part these houses stood on freshly created mountain terraces, flat 'steps' of land dug out of the mountain side. They had already been planted with the season's crops, and we could see that millet and potatoes had begun to grow – not a bad effort so early in March, and at rather more than 7,000 feet. The new plants looked lusciously green and healthy.

The houses we passed appeared to be built of wood, and to be smaller than the traditional village houses, which were usually made from stone. Most of the terraces were quite compact, too, leaving not a lot of space for growing anything, or keeping animals.

Goats wandered about here and there, stretching up and pulling leaves from those trees that had survived the onslaught of man's need to expand, and which still remained standing amongst the newly cut terraces. Water buffalo contemplated life through enormous, gentle, dark eyes from the shade of their new shelters, and chickens strolled here and there, jumping and flapping from terrace to terrace, scratching for seeds with their skinny chicken toes in time honoured, universal chickeny fashion.

The narrow track descended steeply between the terraces – we could have reached out and touched many of the houses as we passed so close to them; an occasional trailing tree branch scraped across the bus windows trying to hold back our descent; and smiling villagers waved and called "Namaste!" to us. We waved back, grinning.

The sun shone, the air reaching us from outside the bus felt pleasantly dry and warm, and a feeling of peacefulness seemed to hang in the atmosphere over this remote, mountainous region.

We very quickly lost our bearings and were unable to work out which way the track was taking us, especially when we realised that we had reached flat land and were driving across the bottom of a narrow, forested valley.

But now we began to ascend the other side, and the bus engine started to scream and screech with the effort of climbing the steep valley wall. We held on to the seats in front of us and tried not to look down at the rolling sea of forest so far below. In no time at all, it seemed, we had staggered bumpily over the crest of the mountain and plunged downwards once again.

Then began a series of mind boggling, stomach lurching switchback turns as the bus stopped and reversed at each one, skidding and skittering from side to side as it got going again and the tyres struggled for traction on the slippy surface.

We eventually reached the bottom of yet another unfamiliar valley and began again the steep climb up the other side. The track was no more than a matter of a foot or so wider than the spread of the bus wheels, and of course there were no safety barriers. We crawled slowly upwards leaving the long shadows of the valley behind us, and moving into the still bright light of a Himalayan evening, as the sun shone down upon us from a clear blue sky that appeared near enough to touch. As we struggled higher the view around us became breath-taking, spectacular, and one that most humans could never forget or grow tired of.

This valley was forested right up to its mountain tops, and the vast number of shades of green in the vegetation and trees shimmered together in the sunlight and rippled in the breeze, turning the whole mountain side into a kaleidoscope of moving greens.

We stared, mesmerised, out of the bus window at the very roof of the world.

The light was beginning to fade as we crawled through what we eventually realised was the rhododendron forest. It had just come into flower, and the rhododendron trees with their massive, gnarled trunks were covered in huge, wonderfully dark red blooms; no surprise then that it is the national flower of Nepal. But I hadn't always felt so affectionate towards the Nepalese rhododendron! This was the very forest we'd had to climb through on several occasions in order to reach or leave the village. To be honest, I should say it was the forest that Tod and Kalyani had had to practically drag me through, and push me up the really steep parts!

Ha! I would never have to suffer that indignity again. But if you'd told me four years ago that one day we'd be traversing the rhododendron forest by bus I wouldn't have believed it. I would probably have *hoped* for it, but I certainly wouldn't have believed it could happen, given the steep remoteness of the terrain.

Suddenly we emerged from the forest and knew exactly where we were. The small village of Lohrimani was in sight towards the far end of the valley which we had now entered, its twenty or thirty wooden houses built haphazardly along the sides of its only road. As the bus approached we became aware of smoke rising straight up into the sky from open, wood fires that burned here and there, and around which villagers sat in gossiping groups. Children played chasing games across the rough, uneven stone surface of the road, giggling and squealing as they ran; and three or four surly canines lay unmoving outside a low, wooden shed set slightly back from the road. From bitter experience I knew that the Lohrimani canines are sly and untrustworthy flea bags, so I was well aware that they were only pretending to ignore the bus as we drove past. Oh yes! I knew without a doubt that they were watching us, sneakily plotting their next move.

Apart from half a dozen new and very attractive stone and wood built houses on its outskirts Lohrimani appeared mostly unchanged, and the bus pulled up outside Kalyani's uncle's shop, a small wooden shed packed with sacks of rice and wonderful smelling herbs. Tod, Kalyani and I had often stopped there on our journeys either to or from Salle, and plonked down to rest on the small wooden bench outside the shop. Nothing had changed; not the shop, not the bench.

Wearily, oh so wearily, we got off the bus in the fast fading light and were immediately swamped by a happy, noisy group of villagers who had come from Salle to meet us. They wanted to say hello, to hug us, and to pull Tod's beard! It was so very good to see them again; after all, this was what we had come half way round the world for.

Kalyani's father, who speaks pretty good English, another couple of her uncles (don't forget that Kalyani holds the world record for having the greatest number of aunts and uncles), and Molly and her son Buddha Llama were all speaking to us at once! We laughed.

They bundled us into the shed next door which had a low wooden table and benches in it. By the dim light inside the one story wooden building we all squeezed, pushed, shoved and giggled our way onto the benches, and in the blink of an eye hot Nepali tea appeared on the table in front of us.

Molly sat down next to me and hugged me so tightly that I could scarcely breathe. We grinned at each other and shook our heads. This lovely lady hadn't changed in the last two years, but I couldn't tell her that as I didn't speak her language and she didn't speak mine. But somehow that had never mattered to us, and we knew that we were friends; friends from vastly different backgrounds and cultures, friends with hugely different life styles, but friends nevertheless. We knew it. We could feel it.

Tod and I drank the tea and looked around. The open fire in the middle of the shed's hard, dry clay floor was the only source of light in the room, and of course it was also the only means of heating the water for tea. One of the village ladies picked a pot of boiling water off the fire, turned and offered it to me. I smiled and shook my head. As she placed the pot back on the fire she said something, and Kalyani's father looked across at me and said,

"She says you are looking older than the last time she saw you," and he smiled and nodded happily, obviously pleased to be the bearer of such good news.

Right-oh. That happens, I suppose. We do all get older.

There could perhaps be an opening for a teacher of Tact and Diplomacy up in the Everest Region of Nepal; possibly a part time position; possibly seasonal work.

But a twenty four hour, seven thousand mile trip, and shortly after that a bumpy, tiring, nail biting twelve hour journey…. Well, that's bound to have added a wrinkle or two here or there, isn't it, unless you're Super Woman? Tod pretended not to have heard, bless him. He knows which side his bread's buttered.

When we had finished our tea another of Kalyani's uncles beckoned us outside, and Kalyani's father told us that we could ride to Salle in a truck if we wanted. Oh wow! Déjà vu! Yes please!

And there it was, waiting for us outside the shop, a brightly painted Indian style truck, complete with massive tyres and grinning driver. Luckily for me it wasn't as big as some other trucks I had encountered in those remote mountainous regions, and this time I managed to scramble into the cab with just a bit of strategically administered help from Tod. The villagers piled into the back of the truck and we got underway with a roar of the engine. Tod and I held on to each other for grim death as we began the slow, steep and bumpy ascent out of the valley, crashing over rocks, skidding on gravel, and dropping heavily down into steep sided gullies along the way. The entire cab shook, trembled and swayed, and we shook, trembled and swayed with it. The noise was deafening.

We reached the top of the ridge above Lohrimani and the track flattened out somewhat there, becoming less steep, and curving around the top of the mountain before heading down into the next valley, 'our' valley. At long last we were within sight of the village again.

Minutes later the truck stopped and we scrambled out, jumping down onto the track and standing there together in silence, gazing out from the edge of the mountain over the valley towards the village. We were instantly shocked to see how much of the once thick and vibrant forest, which had once virtually surrounded Salle, had vanished. Bare mountain terraces now rose up all around the village with hardly more than a couple of trees in sight.

My heart sank and I just couldn't help thinking,

"How will they feed the animals? What will they use for fuel? How will they light fires for cooking and keeping warm?"

Tod and I looked at each other in silence and I knew that his thoughts mirrored my own. But we were aware that we couldn't dwell on the uncertainties of Salle's future at that moment; we couldn't allow ourselves to fret about the impending, inevitable fight for survival facing the village; not just then. That would come later, much later; after our visit.

I can't tell you how good it was to finally climb down the familiar, steep path into the village, and stop in front of Kalyani's parents' house. We were back once again!

The little group of villagers that had accompanied us stood around laughing and chatting, and Kalyani's mother, alerted by the kerfuffle outside her door, rushed out of the house and hugged us both. That lovely lady didn't seem to have changed one little bit since we had last seen her, and she positively beamed at us.

Grandfather, hearing the commotion, appeared in the doorway of his house nearby, and came over as fast as he could to greet us. He hugged Tod again and again. Then he grabbed my hand, touched my face, and hugged me too. I noticed that he had lost the sight in an eye since we had last seen him. We had brought him a pair of glasses then and he had been thrilled, using them for any close work he was doing, and for checking on his bees. I wondered if his sight loss was due to some relatively 'simple' problem that could easily be fixed if only he lived in some other country where expert medical treatment was available, affordable, within reach, and didn't involve trekking over mountains and down valleys to get to it. An uncomfortable feeling, a chilling mixture of guilt and sadness, made me blink back sudden tears. Nevertheless, despite his obvious problem Grandfather still seemed to have retained his old vitality and sense of humour, and he quickly made us feel genuinely welcome in his village once again.

We were tired. The villagers had put our heavy rucksacks upstairs from where we stood, in Kalyani's old room, and now they ushered us up the unstable, external ladder on to the wooden veranda above the door to Kalyani's parents' house. Everything seemed just the same as it had been two years before, even the ladder swayed and slipped, creaked and groaned, in just the same scary way!

Kalyani's father had unrolled a rug across the room's uneven wooden floor – we instantly remembered it from our last visit. It was the only one in the village, perhaps in the whole region, and had been carried up to Salle especially for Kalyani. We took our walking boots off and stepped into the small room. The thick, blue, patterned rug felt refreshingly soft beneath our trekking socks.

Nothing had changed. It was absolutely *not* a typical village room. The table, bookcase and low wooden bed with the wooden slats in place of a mattress were still all there. When Kalyani had lived at home, at the time we had first stayed in the village, she had been headmistress of the village school, and was the only villager to possess, or have any use at all for a table and bookcase. They, like the rug, had been brought up to the village specially. There were even two wooden chairs next to the table.

Our rucksacks had been placed in a corner of the room, and we saw that on the floor beside them were two plates of hard boiled eggs and freshly prepared chips. How wonderful! Kalyani's Mum had remembered! We had just about *lived* on hard boiled eggs and chips during the five months of our first visit to Salle. We munched gratefully, not realising how hungry we were.

Several of the villagers had followed us into the room and now sat on the floor watching us, smiling. I suppose they think that most English people have rather strange diets, and a particular penchant for hard boiled eggs. Oh dear.

Then, one by one they stood up, wished us a good night, and left us. We heard them shushing each other and laughing as they softly closed the door. The ladder rattled and creaked, shoeless footsteps padded away across the hard baked clay outside the house, and the peaceful silence of night in the high Himalayas gently descended on the village.

Wearily we laid our coats across the wooden slats and climbed onto the bed, pulling the cover over us, knowing that the night would be cold indeed. We were asleep even before the first night hunting bird flew over the village, its eerie call echoing out across the valley through the fast falling darkness.

CHAPTER SIX

We heard the sound of children's voices as the first light of a new Himalayan day began to sidle in through the cracks in the wooden shutters over the glassless windows. The unfamiliar objects in our room began to emerge in strange shapes from the gloom around us, and we blinked, yawned, and sat up. Well, Tod did.

They were gathering below the small, wooden balcony outside our room, chattering and laughing, running about and chasing the long suffering chickens who squawked indignantly and raced for cover. I didn't blame them. A Himalayan chicken does not have an easy life.

The kids were waiting for us to emerge from our room so they could shout,

"Hello! Hello!" at us as loudly as they could, and of course they were waiting to see what goodies we had brought for them in those heavy, enticingly bulky rucksacks we'd lugged all the way from England!

I won't spend too much time whingeing about my aching back and sore legs! (I may already have mentioned somewhere that I have single handedly raised whingeing to an art form). But an uncomfortable night spent on a rock hard bed, with my jacket lining for a pillow and a lumpy cover to keep the cold away was doubtless to blame for my seized up joints; that, and the fact that the bus journey had taken twelve tiring hours.

Suffice to say it really wasn't one of my better mornings. Tentatively I lowered a set of toes towards the rug, peering short sightedly down into the gloom, anxious to make sure that my toes, when they arrived at their destination would be alone there.

By the time I'd staggered about the room moaning and groaning, found my clothes and given them a good shake in case someone else was already in there, checked out, and

41

then pulled my walking boots on, I felt a bit better. Just a *bit*.

We opened the rough wooden shutters that passed as a door and stepped over the threshold onto the balcony. I smiled as I remembered the number of times I'd actually tripped and fallen out onto the balcony. No such indignity today, thank goodness.

The sun had just risen and the air that greeted us was warm, fresh, and indefinably different to the air anywhere else in the world. What was it, I wondered, that made the air up in these magnificently rugged mountains so wonderfully unlike the air elsewhere?

I gazed out across the valley that swept away into the distance below us, at the village houses scattered here and there, at the many terraces of different sizes looking for all the world like giant steps leading up to the mountain ridges high above. But where were the trees? Their absence from the landscape simply screamed out at us. We could have been looking at a totally different valley to the forested one that we remembered from our previous visits.

Of course Tod was disgustingly bright and smiley as usual that morning, and as soon as the kids saw him they squealed and raced up the rickety ladder to join us. The balcony swayed and creaked ominously under the onslaught, and I felt the first worry of the day coming on. Would it hold everyone who wanted to sit on it? Or would it have the last laugh and dump us all on the hard clay ground below? Oh dear.

The kids jumped around laughing, pulling Tod's beard and practising their English on us. The happy cacophony attracted other villagers, who came to see what was going on, and stood together in groups below the balcony, smiling up at us. We recognised nearly everyone.

I noticed that although these kids were village children who we knew from our previous visits, there were none of 'our' class amongst them; none of the ten children we had taught at the village school.

How strange. Where were they all, I wondered? It was a national festival that day and all the schools were closed, but even so we couldn't see any of our class of 2009.

Kalyani's mother climbed into the room behind us through a kind of wooden hatchway that opened from her house below. She came over to the balcony and shooed the kids away. They went in a hurry, shrieking with laughter, rushing and tumbling down the ladder, and joining the adults on the ground below.

Kalyani's mother took our hands and pulled us back into the room. She closed the shutters against the noise of what had become a bit of a party outside her house. By the dim light in the room we saw she had laid Nepali tea and boiled eggs on the floor, lovingly prepared for us over the open fire in the middle of the hard clay floor downstairs. We thanked her. She is a truly kind and thoughtful woman, a mother hen whose caring nature could translate into any other culture. We are very fond of Kalyani's mother.

After breakfast we began the major job of unpacking our rucksacks and organising the gifts. We hoped we had brought something for everyone. The most acceptable gifts for the village ladies were always soap, hair shampoo, and thermal underwear; and thermal vests and socks for the men. This time we had crammed towels and face flannels in too, and a whole assortment of other goodies, including fleece jackets and books, pens and crayons for the children. I wondered how much they had grown in the last two years, and worried that the fleeces might not fit them.

We had no idea when Kalyani would arrive, and until she did we had no way of discovering where 'our' class had got to. We would just have to be patient.

The noise from outside the house had abated somewhat. The adults seemed to have returned to their work on the terraces or elsewhere in the village, and the children's squeals and laughter had quietened down – always a bad sign!

We pretended not to notice when the shutters were pushed slowly open and one by one the children slid quietly into the room and sat together on the floor. They whispered, giggled and watched us in fascination.

Kalyani's room is no more than 10ft by 12ft, but you'd be amazed at just how many small Nepalese children can pack in on the floor and still leave room for Tod and me to pile clothes, pens, hair shampoo, soap, towels, toothpaste, books, games, and much more onto the bed.

We had just emptied the rucksacks and a number of smaller bags, and established some kind of order amongst the gifts to be distributed when a familiar, much loved voice suddenly shouted from behind us,

"Tod! Fiona! I am here at last!"

We turned and saw our Little Ant, Kalyani, standing grinning broadly in the doorway. She looked radiant, silhouetted against the morning sunshine, her hair pulled back from her face, pashmina around her shoulders. What an entrance! Entirely worthy of a screen diva!

"Kalyani!" Tod and I yelled, thrilled to see her again.

The carpet of small children at our feet scurried apart as if by magic to let Kalyani, Tod and I rush together and grab each other in a group hug. We were all talking at once, so pleased to have met up again after two years.

Kalyani was hot and out of breath. She had come as quickly as she could from her husband's village to join us, and had been walking through the mountains since first light.

When we finally emerged from our hug and sat down on the floor together, we noticed that one or two of the children were crying silently, and Kalyani's mother, who had followed her daughter into the room and sat down quietly in a corner, was sobbing.

We had kept in touch with Kalyani since the first time we'd met in 2009, when Tod and I had spent five months or so in Nepal. We'd managed to reach her by mobile phone at least two or three times a month since then.

We already knew that she had applied for a Visa to join her husband in Australia, but when she told us now that the Visa would be through any day, we were shocked. It was really going to happen. Our Little Ant was moving on.

She didn't yet have a plane ticket, and didn't know what date she would be able to travel, but Kalyani wanted us to spend time with her in Kathmandu before she left for Australia. And she was sure that would be within days. Tod and I were stunned.

We were already two days later than planned in our itinerary because of the strikes, and we were due to go south, to Chitwan, to see our friend Karma in a day or two. But we said yes to Kalyani. Of course we said yes.

We agreed to leave the village and return to Kathmandu with her the very next day. We felt sad already. A sense of loss hovered over us, depressed us. I looked across the room at Kalyani's mother – she was still sobbing quietly, wiping her eyes with the corner of her pashmina. My heart went out to her.

But for now we needed the answer to the riddle of our disappearing class of 2009! So we asked Kalyani where they all were. And so it was that we discovered just how much had changed in the life of the village since we had last been there in 2011.

Kalyani told us that the village school where we had taught English and sport, and had so much fun, had been demolished and rebuilt further up the mountainside. It was bigger now, with a much increased intake of children.

'Our' class from the village school had dispersed, with some of the children moving on to the local state school where Kalyani's father was head teacher, some leaving school completely, and some moving out of the area, either to study elsewhere, or accompanying their parents who had found work in other regions.

Sadly, Kalyani herself had lost touch with most of our class.

But right on cue there was a shout from outside, and our lovely Parbatti positively leapt through the door and grabbed Tod and me, laughing and sobbing at one and the same time. We hugged her, delighted to see her again.

Parbatti is a wonderful, bright, shy and softly spoken girl who was in our class. The last time we had seen her, in 2011, she had been standing on a rough track in an isolated valley, outside her family house, waving goodbye to us as we walked with Kalyani to visit her parents in law in another valley.

Parbatti had watched us go, waving and crying silently until we turned a bend in the track and lost sight of her.

That image of Parbatti, a lovely young girl standing alone against the stark, rugged background of the Himalayas, tears streaming down her face as she waved goodbye to us, has never left us. It has a special place in our memories. Whenever I think of Parbatti that is how I remember her.

Friends of ours in England, Sue and her granddaughters, have 'adopted' Parbatti, and have sent her letters and presents over the years. We had brought bags of goodies with us from Sue and the girls to give to Parbatti and her best friend Susila. The bags were hiding somewhere amongst the piles of gifts now spread out on the bed, and Tod began rooting around, searching for them.

We asked Parbatti about her family and her schooling. She had been attending the state school for the last few years and was still uncomplainingly walking up to four hours a day to get there and back. She had never missed a day. She told us her family were all well, and that she was still enjoying school, and still doing well there.

Eventually, the tears that had been running down Parbatti's face constantly since she arrived in the room stopped, and I gave her a handkie to wipe her eyes with.

But then Tod managed to find the presents from Sue's girls. He handed the heavy, bulky bag to Parbatti, and told her who it was from. If the look of astonishment and pleasure that appeared on Parbatti's face could have been bottled, it would have lit up the whole of Nepal for a year. She sobbed, sitting there on the floor with the unopened bag on her lap, her tears making little damp patches as they fell on it. I handed her another handkie.

Now our Ant was definitely at the very back of the queue when 'patience' was given out, and as Parbatti was being rather slow opening up her presents Kalyani reached across, grabbed the bag, pulled it open and began rummaging in it.

Total silence fell upon the room as she did so. All eyes gazed fixedly at the bag, and all breath was held as Kalyani started pulling out the goodies one by one. The 'oohs' and 'aahhs' grew louder as the goodies mounted up, and when the large, brown envelope containing photos of Sue and her girls came out, Kalyani and Parbatti were instantly swamped by a mass of squealing, giggling children as they all scrambled over and tried to look at the photos at the same time.

Laughing, Tod and I tried to bring some order to the scrum. We rescued Parbatti's presents for her, scrabbling around on the floor until we had them all safely back in the bag, and then we asked Kalyani to tell the kids that we had brought something for everyone – no one would leave without a present, and that went for the adults too.

However, we judged it prudent not to give Parbatti the presents *we* had brought for her just at that moment. She looked rather shell shocked, and was quietly opening up and reading through the letters Sue's girls had sent her, occasionally asking Kalyani to translate a word or two.

47

In the absence of any other member of our class of 2009 we decided on a plan of action. With Kalyani's help we filled half a dozen bags with a variety of goodies and clearly marked on them the names of the children Kalyani knew were still in the area. Kalyani's father agreed to find the children and deliver the bags to them. Job done!

That left us with a pile of goodies ready and waiting to be distributed. Ha!

By that time the room was absolutely packed to the rafters with villagers old and young. Men, women and children squished together on the floor like happy sardines, and overflowed out through the shutters onto the rickety balcony. The sound of their laughter floated out across the valley.

I felt another worry coming on. Would the floor collapse under their weight?

We saw several villagers in the throng that we specially wanted to talk to. Molly had come in, and Susila's grandfather, the yak milkman, was there too. Incidentally, there is nothing quite as tasty as fresh yak milk. The next time you happen to be hanging around when a yak is being milked, do try to sample some. You won't regret it. Kalyani's sister Laxmi was there; half a dozen village men had come in to say hello to Tod; and of course grandfather and grandmother had arrived.

Kalyani's mum was still sitting in a corner of the room talking, and wiping away the occasional tear. It seemed that her happiness for Kalyani's impending new life was weighed almost equally against her sorrow at losing her daughter. I wondered grimly what her chances were of visiting Kalyani in Australia. Not good, I feared.

We were ready. Tod and I grinned at each other, took deep breaths, and began distributing the gifts.

CHAPTER SEVEN

That afternoon was great fun, with smiles and laughter being the order of the day. There we were, squashed in a small room, in a small village, high in the remote Everest region of Nepal, just about a whisker away from the mighty Everest, and we couldn't have enjoyed ourselves more!

Kalyani helped us make sure that everyone in the room got a gift, and took something away with them, no matter how small, for others in their family.

The hair shampoo and soap were probably the most popular items, but the socks, hair clips and watches ran them a close second.

This time, having checked beforehand that it would be acceptable, we'd brought some make up for the girls. Kalyani took charge of the distribution, oohing and aahing at the eye shadows and nail varnish colours, and pinching a couple of the brightest ones for herself! We all laughed.

The quiet and gentle village lady who had given us 'Lucky' the cockerel on our last visit (to my absolute horror!) wasn't able to join us. She was ill, but she had sent her eldest daughter and youngest son to say hello to us. The children stood together timidly at the back of the room holding hands in silence. We had brought a warm pullover for the little boy, working on the assumption that he would have grown somewhat in the intervening two years. But actually he didn't seem to have grown at all, and was still the small, adorable, shy boy he'd been then. The pullover, when we put it on him, hung down to his knees! Not to worry, he'd grow into it. Probably.

The little lad made his way over to Tod and stood leaning against his leg, smiling shyly up at him. I spotted the tell-tale glint of a bit of a tear in Tod's eye as he looked down and tousled the youngster's hair.

We sent a bag full of goodies to the young boy's mother and quite a bit of money too. She was still bringing up nine children without a husband, and therefore without an income. Her husband had become very ill a few years ago, not long before we first set foot in the village, and as a result he had committed suicide. As shocking as that may seem to our Western sensitivities, it is not uncommon in the remote regions of Nepal. Medical help is often out of the reach of many villagers, who may simply not be able to access that help given the inaccessible nature of the terrain. And of course any medical help has to be paid for.

I asked Kalyani who the two lovely young girls sitting quietly together in a corner were,

"You *know* who they are!" Kalyani laughed, "They are the youngsters from the house next to where you lived in 2009!"

"No!" Tod and I both said together, amazed. We couldn't believe it. These were the two veritable tomboys who had been a constant presence outside, and often inside our room four years ago!

On one occasion they had climbed the tree outside at the back of the house and thrown hard, unripe peaches through our glassless window! We had taken cover from the bombardment as unripe missiles crashed into the wooden floor and onto the table, scattering papers around and knocking water bottles over. When the girls eventually ran out of ammunition we came out of hiding and asked them why they had done it, why they had bombarded us! They very sweetly told us that they knew from their school lessons that English people liked fruit, but they thought that, as we were old, we might not have been able to climb the tree to get it!

They had danced and sung for us in the evenings after school, using the area of flat, hardened clay outside the front of the house as their stage, with the deep green valley and high mountain range behind it as their backdrop.

The girls attended the small, state school in the village of Lohrimani, and they took every opportunity to practice the English that they learned there. Unlike the children in our class, these youngsters were not shy, and were not embarrassed to 'have a go' in English. They were loud, sweet and funny, and they made us laugh. We loved them.

Now here they were all grown up, and so far removed from their tomboy behaviour of the past that they positively drooled over the make-up and nail varnish, and grabbed the hair clips and shampoo with gusto!

The village yak and buffalo milk man came over to shake our hands and give us the cups of fresh milk he had brought. His granddaughter is Susila, Parbatti's best friend, and another of our class of 2009. From him, with Kalyani translating, we learned that Susila was now studying at a school in a village thirty miles away. As she was living there during term time she hadn't been able to travel back to see us. We were disappointed.

In 2009 Susila had a strange rash all over the lower part of her legs. Her mother asked us if we could cure it, so we took photos of the rash, and I eventually asked my Doctor in the UK if she knew what it was. The answer was that it seemed to be some kind of fungal infection, and when we returned to the village in 2011 we took with us a possible cure for it. We left the special soap with Susila, and explained that she should apply it to her legs every day. Now her grandfather told us that the rash had completely cleared up, and he wanted to thank us. We were really pleased for Susila, knowing how self-conscious she had been about the rash.

We gave Parbatti a bag of goodies for Susila, plus the presents that Sue and her girls had sent. Parbatti was planning on visiting her friend very soon, and promised to deliver the presents in the next few days.

51

We had brought a lovely, frilly, pink baby girl tee shirt for Laxmi's baby, and handed it over to her with soap and shampoo. Laxmi held the tee shirt up for the room to view, and there was much oohing and aahing in admiration. But oops! Bit of a bloomer! The baby was a boy! I'm not sure how we'd somehow changed its gender, but Laxmi was thrilled anyway, and stuck the tee shirt on her baby right away.

Our friend Carolyn had sent half a dozen absolutely beautiful baby outfits, and word of their arrival had already gone out to the families of the three tiny new additions to the village. The mothers and babies arrived and we brought out the new clothes. The women were thrilled, and the outfits were passed around the room and much admired. Whether they liked it or not, and one or two didn't, the babies were duly dressed in their new clothes and held up for a photo opportunity!

Throughout the afternoon the room filled up with freshly picked rhododendron flowers, and countless bottles of Raxi, the local home brewed firewater. Most of the villagers have some in their houses, and this is really the only present they can give us. No one came empty handed. We politely thanked everyone, took each container and stood them all in a row at the side of the room. Later, when we left the village, we asked Kalyani's Mum to give them back, and apologise that we hadn't had time to drink them!

The children had spent quite some time collecting the beautiful, red rhododendron flowers from the mountain side and patiently weaving them into traditional garlands. They hung them round the room, and the aroma, although not strong, was pleasantly noticeable.

Grandfather came in with some honey he'd just liberated from his bees. He is such a kind hearted man and knows that Tod keeps bees too, although there would seem to be but few points of comparison between bee keeping in rural England, and bee keeping high in the Himalayas of

Nepal. Nevertheless the pair always exchanged the latest information, with Kalyani translating, and Tod and I loved to go with grandfather to see how his bees were getting on. But, as with the Raxi, we asked Kalyani's Mum to return the honey to grandfather with our apologies after we had left. We knew we would not have time to eat it, and we also knew how very precious and rare honey was up there in such a high and isolated place.

Grandmother tried it on again! What a woman! I made a point of giving her quite a substantial goody bag early on in the day, but later, with a tear in her eye, she told Kalyani that we'd forgotten her. Believe it or not she did exactly the same thing two years previously! She has obviously missed her vocation – she should have been an actor. But we all played along, apologised profusely trying not to grin, and gave her more soap and shampoo to go with the thermal vests we had already given her!

The daylight eventually faded and our room gradually emptied. We suddenly realised it had been raining all day. We stood on the balcony gazing out over the valley, watching the shadows lengthen as the sun sank behind the mountains, turning them into dark and formidable guardians of the roof of the world.

Molly invited us to her house, as she had done each time we'd visited the village. So Tod and I, Kalyani, Molly and her son traipsed through the damp, rolling mist over the nearby mountain ridge and down the rocky slope to the little house with the fantastic view over the valley.

Molly's son Buddha Llama thanked us for the large bag of dog biscuits we'd brought, and then positively forced his elderly dog to munch a couple of them in front of us. I felt sorry for the creature; too many biscuits, munched too fast, may cause canine hiccups. But I hadn't forgotten that this is the mutt who attacked poor old Woolly Dog on the occasion he followed us to school. I could still picture the dog launching himself off the steep hillside onto Woolly's back on the narrow track below, his white, pointy teeth gnashing. I glared at him. He glared back. No love lost there.

To be honest, the intended destination for our bag of dog biscuits was not in fact Buddha Llama's elderly dog. We had hoped to see 'Son of Woolly' again, and asked Kalyani where he was. We were saddened when she told us that Son of Woolly had left the village and she didn't know where he was. She told us that the family, outside whose house he had lived, had stopped feeding him,

"But *why*?" I said, hoping I wasn't going to start crying, "Why on earth did they stop?"

"Because they have a baby now and not enough food for the dog too," Kalyani said quietly, studiously avoiding looking at me. I stared hard at her, wondering if that was the truth; wondering if the truth was really much worse; wondering if I could bear it.

Before we had left Kathmandu to travel up to the village we had spoken to Kalyani on the phone a couple of times. During one of our conversations she had told us that Molly's water buffalo had recently been killed by a wild tiger that had come into the village hunting for food. Knowing that Molly's buffalo had only just had a baby, we assumed that it was in fact the baby that had been killed. But we were wrong. The tiger had killed the mother water buffalo, and those of you who have any idea of the size and strength of a water buffalo will realise that the tiger must indeed have been a large, strong and determined creature to overcome a female water buffalo protecting her baby.

Molly's terrace, where she grows millet and potatoes, and keeps her water buffalo in a shelter made from bamboo, is across the village, and quite some distance from her house. There was therefore no possibility that her elderly dog could have heard or scented the tiger and warned the villagers of the presence of the dangerous intruder.

On many occasions in the past Woolly Dog and other village dogs, alerted to the stealthy approach of a hunting tiger in the darkness of a Himalayan night, had set up such a barrage of barking and snarling that the tiger had retreated. That was the dogs' job. That was what they did.

Alas, the treatment consistently meted out to the Himalayan canine has been nothing short of shamefully atrocious in Nepal. Despite providing loyal protection for villagers and livestock alike, the dogs are generally unloved, frequently despised, and most certainly unappreciated. It is rare in the extreme that any human, adult or child, will even reach out to touch a dog. They are treated for the most part like undesirable vermin, and are frequently beaten for no reason at the drop of a hat. If they are fed at all by humans it is with meagre scraps of waste thrown out of the house. It goes without saying that the dogs are afraid of humans. They inhabit a sad, dark and miserable hinterland in Nepal, having evolved to the point where they are no longer 'wild' creatures as such, but not to the point of domestic acceptability by humans.

So where are they to go? What are they to do?

There is now only one dog remaining in the entire village of Salle.

CHAPTER EIGHT

Molly makes the best Raxi in the village! She adds a secret ingredient which seems to be some kind of herb; at least, that's what they have always told us! Tod and I both sampled some, sitting on the floor in Molly's house that evening, chatting with her and Kalyani by the light of the open fire in the middle of the room. To say that Raxi is strong is an understatement, but it would certainly clean up any old coins you may have, or happily remove the paint from the wing of your car, should you wish to respray it.

By the time we said goodnight to Molly and her son, and walked back through the darkness to our room we were yawning. It had been a busy and emotional day. We got ready for bed by the light of a torch, rolling our pullovers up tightly and pushing our socks into our boots, hoping to outwit any nocturnal wanderer with no sense of smell, and settled down under the cover. There was complete silence in the house, and across the village. Everyone had gone to bed. We lay staring wide eyed into the darkness, waiting for sleep.

Suddenly I heard a sound. It seemed to be coming from the ceiling. I listened, and heard it again,

"Tod!" I whispered, "Can you hear that?"

Silence,

"Tod!" and I jabbed an elbow in his direction just in case he hadn't heard me,

"What?" he mumbled, "Hear what?"

I do think he's getting rather deaf, but obligingly the sound came again. It was a series of sharp little tapping noises which stopped for a few seconds and then began again. It was definitely coming from overhead, and seemed to be moving around above us.

"What's that?" I asked, "Is someone up there?" and I stared anxiously upwards through the darkness,

"Some*thing*," Tod mumbled,

"What?" I squeaked as quietly as I could, "What do you mean 'some*thing*'?" and I shuffled up onto an elbow and glared in his direction,

"I mean 'some*thing*' is up there, not 'some*one*,'" Tod said, his voice still muffled by the cover,

"What are you talking about?" I said, feeling peeved, and I jabbed him again, "Listen to that! Someone's up there!"

He chuckled. He *actually* chuckled! And then reached out and picked up the torch from the floor at the side of the bed,

"If that's a person up there he'd have fallen through the ceiling by now!" he said, rather too smugly I thought, "That plywood wouldn't hold *anyone's* weight," and he switched the torch on and directed the bright beam upwards.

It illuminated most of a low ceiling divided into four roughly equal squares. Three of the squares were covered by sheets of thin plywood with Nepali writing on them in one or two of the corners, but the fourth square was covered only by a piece of sagging blue plastic, looking rather like a large, thick plastic bag, roughly taped to the plywood either side of it.

The sound came again,

"It's a mouse!" I giggled, feeling relieved.

The tiny paw steps moved around on the plywood, running here, pausing there, and eventually reaching the section of plastic. Here the sound changed, and Tod shone the torch on the blue plastic just in time to catch our visitor's progress across it – the plastic bulged downwards considerably, making a kind of dull, crunching sound as the unknown trekker crossed it!

"Humm!" Tod said, "Looks like quite a chunky mouse!"

Oh no! I wondered what the next size up from a mouse was there in Nepal. Oh dear. I hoped whatever it was wasn't going to fall through the plastic.

Better not dwell on that thought, I decided, or I'd never get to sleep.

We followed the creature's progress for quite a while, wondering what it was doing up there, giggling and remembering a similar encounter we had had on our first visit to the village. On that occasion a mouse seemed to have been responsible for the 'removal' of a family of poisonous spiders.

Eventually the noises stopped, and we turned off the torch and went to sleep. Silence settled across the village and our room,

"Tod!"

"What?"

"What's that?"

"What?"

"That noise!"

"What noise?"

"A sort of 'paper crinkling' noise!"

The sound was coming from inside the room this time,

"That sounds like….umm….it sounds like…." Tod said,

"Like *what*? What does it sound like?" I squeaked, "It's *here,* in the room!"

"Oh yes, I know what it is!" Tod said, "It's the packet of biscuits we brought from Kathmandu. It's wrapped in thick, really crinkly paper. I left it on the floor next to our rucksacks."

"What!" I almost shouted, instantly glad that Tod was on the side of the bed nearest to the noisy biscuits, "What's happening to them?"

"Dunno," he said, and grabbed the torch again, switching it on and spraying the beam along the side of the room. It shot fast moving black fingers of shadow in front

of it, and illuminated our rucksacks and a dozen bottles of Raxi standing in a row on the floor, like miniature soldiers. Nothing moved. The noise had stopped,
"Can you see the packet of biscuits?" I whispered.
"Nope. It's on the other side of the rucksack," Tod said, "But there's nothing there. Let's go back to sleep," and he put out the torch and settled down again.
I was horrified,
"But what if it's something dangerous?" I whinged, "What if it's hanging around, being....dangerous?"
"Like a biscuit eating tiger, you mean?" Tod said.
I do sometimes think that his humour can be somewhat misplaced, even facetious, so I elbowed him in the ribs and pulled the cover over my head. I'd heard enough noises for one night. *He* was on the biscuit side of the bed so *he* could deal with it, whatever it was.

'Lucky' the cockerel woke us early the next morning, cock a doodle doing loudly through the darkness. We both laughed as we heard Kalyani shout,
"Quiet!"
Her mother had adopted Lucky two years ago after he had been given to us, destined for the pot, *our* pot! She provided him with a small wooden hutch to sleep in outside the door to her house, and fed him rice every day. Lucky rewarded her by waking her, and half the village, every morning considerably earlier than dawn. Although he didn't know it, he continued to avoid the pot simply by merit of 'belonging' to Tod and me! Mind you, we were not absolutely sure that Lucky **had** avoided the pot, and it did actually cross our minds that the glossy cockerel strutting around outside the house may in fact have been an imposter, and one who perhaps enjoyed a bit more of a lie-in in the mornings than Lucky did. But if he **was** an imposter, he'd drunk from the same 'get up far too early and make loud cockerel noises' bottle too!

It seemed much more likely that Kalyani's mother, being the kind hearted woman that she was, had taken to wearing ear plugs,

"It's good to hear Lucky enjoying life!" Tod said, and I gave him a suspicious glance. Hummm, was this the same Tod who had once described Lucky as 'a bunch of coloured feathers with attitude'?

Oh well, we were awake, so I bumbled about finding my glasses and getting dressed, and then started to pack the few belongings that we had with us. It seemed strange to have so little to carry; strange but nice.

Tod opened the shutters onto the balcony and stood gazing out across the valley. Warm air, pleasantly perfumed with incense, crept into the room, along with the fragile early morning sunlight.

I finished shoving odds and ends into a rucksack and looked around to see what we had forgotten. But apart from the bottles of Raxi, grandfather's honey and our rucksacks there was now nothing else on the floor,

"Did you pick those biscuits up?" I asked Tod's back, looking round for them, "The crinkly ones. I hope you've thrown them out. The chickens will probably eat them."

I sat down on the edge of the bed and looked over at Tod. He hadn't responded, but he *had* turned to face me. We stared at each other,

"So, you didn't pick them up?" I said, "Huummm! Where do you suppose they are then?" and we both looked round the room, under the small table, in the corners, under the bed, and finally, just for good measure, up to the ceiling.

They were there. At least, part of the crinkly paper packet was there. Sticking out from a hole in a corner of the ceiling. We stared at each other,

"That was quite a heavy packet of biscuits," I said, "Heavy, that is, if you're a mouse."

"Umm," Tod nodded, "Must have been a strong little bugger to carry it up there!" he said thoughtfully, and we stared at each other again. Hanging between us, unspoken, was the scary possibility that our 'mouse' was in fact its cousin – the next size up.

I was very glad that we were not spending another night in that room. I did not wish to lie in bed staring up at the ceiling in the darkness, listening to an unspecified member of the rodent family munching through its ill-gotten gains.

Shortly after, Kalyani's mother brought us breakfast. We sat on the balcony eating and watching village life get underway. It was late spring, a busy time of year, and both crops and animals needed attention. We could see villagers already working on their terraces, digging or ploughing with water buffalo.

Kalyani came out of the house below us,

"We will go in ten minutes," she called, "Are you ready?"

"Yes, just give us a couple of minutes," I said, and walked back into the room to pick up our rucksacks. Tod followed me. I swung my arms into the straps, and pulled the rucksack onto my back easily as it was so light. I turned and looked at Tod to see where he was up to. He was just leaning over fastening the top of his rucksack which stood on the floor in front of him.

I saw it because Tod was leaning over. I saw it on the rough stone wall behind him. It was so big that I thought it couldn't possibly be real. I thought it was some kind of wall ornament, a wood carving maybe. But then it moved,

"Oh my God!" I whispered, "Tod, come over here, *fast!*" and I reached out, grabbed his arm and gave it a tug. He looked up in surprise, saw my expression, and stepped quickly towards me before turning round to look behind him.

He saw it immediately. You could not have missed it.

The spider was pale in colour, almost cream, and must have measured a good nine inches across, from the tip of one gangly leg, across the flat body, to the tip of another gangly leg on the other side. We had never encountered an arachnid like this one. I didn't even know they made them that big. It took my breath away, and I shivered. I suppose its mother must have loved it, but the only thing it had going for it as far as *I* was concerned was that it was moving so slowly as to be almost motionless. I stared at it.

It wasn't that I suspected it was going to rush us, so I needed to keep an eye on it, but I really felt as if I'd turned to stone, and simply *couldn't* drag my gaze away from the monster.

Tod moved over to the balcony and looked down. Kalyani's younger brother was standing there outside the house waiting for us, ready to return to Kathmandu. Tod called to him and beckoned him to come upstairs. I suppose the young lad thought we needed help with our rucksacks or some such thing, and he positively bounded up the ladder and into the room, grinning broadly. He stopped dead when he saw the look on my face, and his eyes followed my pointing hand, widening slightly when he saw what it indicated,

"Ah!" he said, "A spider!" and his grin faded somewhat.

Yes indeedy; a spider,

"Wait, wait," the young lad said in our direction, and shot off back down the ladder. We heard him shouting something, and then he was back again, clutching a thin plastic carrier bag such as is available in most supermarkets. This one had Nepali writing on it.

"Ok," he said, and dropping to his knees he flattened the plastic bag out on the floor in front of him, smoothing his hands over it, attempting to remove the crinkles. Then he folded it neatly in half, and flattened it out again.

We watched in polite, interested silence; Tod, me and the spider.

Kalyani's brother stood up, adjusted the bag in his hand, and walked over to the now completely immobile monster on the wall. With hardly a pause he brought the folded bag up and placed it completely over the spider, lifting the creature off the wall, and holding it in the plastic bag, obviously so that he didn't have to touch it. He then turned and headed for the balcony. Our last view of the spider was of several of its legs dangling out below the bag. I shuddered. He released it in front of the house, and we heard Kalyani scream as it shot past her into the undergrowth and out of sight.

No one knew if the spider was poisonous, but we had seen several cases of spider bites in the past, and they had all been very nasty, and very painful. Goodness knows how a bite from an arachnid of *that* size would make you feel,

"I hope there aren't any more of them around," I said nervously, checking the floor and walls for any sign of life,

"No, there won't be," Tod said confidently, "That one was just an opportunist."

"I don't *care* what religion it was," I told him, "I hope I never see one like it again!"

Kalyani, Tod and I said a tearful farewell to the villagers, especially to Kalyani's mother who kissed us and hugged us tightly, and to father and grandfather. We had no idea when we would see them again, if ever. Grandfather put his arms around Tod and me, and told us that he prayed he would see us again before he died.

Then we left the village in the bright sunshine of a perfect Himalayan morning, with garlands of fresh flowers round our necks, and a fingerprint of tikka on our foreheads to keep us safe on our travels. It was in fact the third time we had left the village of Salle.

We walked to Lohrimani where for the first time ever we could take a bus back to Kathmandu, and not have to climb through the rhododendron forest, and up the mountain to Cowah. I use the verb 'climb' rather loosely in my case.

Parbatti was waiting in Lohrimani to see us off, standing quietly at the spot where we would board the bus. She hugged us, and began to cry. She made us promise to thank Sue and her grandchildren for all the presents, and thanked us again for the gifts and money we had given her and her family.

Bicass, a happy, friendly boy from our class was also waiting there to see us. He had not been able to come to the village yesterday as he was working, but we had sent a bag of gifts to him. He was wearing the fleece pullover we'd brought for him, and we were so glad that it fitted him! He loved it, and wanted to thank us.

We sat down outside the low wooden shed where we'd had Nepali tea on our arrival two days previously. Bicass and Parbatti joined us and chatted shyly with us in English.

An assortment of villagers, children, and Kalyani's aunts and uncles milled around on the rough track through the village, waving to us and wishing us good luck.

Molly appeared and hugged us. She had followed us from Salle. She touched my face and asked Kalyani to thank us both for coming back to the village, for remembering them.

Then the bus arrived in a flurry of dust and screeching brakes, and we got on, Tod, Kalyani and I, all of us close to tears.

Parbatti stood outside the bus window by our seat looking miserable. Every so often she looked up and waved to us. We waved back, trying to smile.

The bus engine roared into life, smothering everyone standing around in thick, black smoke from its exhaust. As the bus began to move off we heard Parbatti shout,

"Fiona! Tod!" and we craned round in our seats to wave again; to wave a last goodbye to her. She was crying.

We concentrated in silence on the scenery outside the bus windows - the rhododendron forest, the new village outside Cowah, the rugged beauty of the Himalayas - each wrapped in our own thoughts.

An hour later we stopped in the small village of Maina Pokhari for five minutes, to pick up more travellers.

I jumped in fright as someone banged on the window next to me. It was Susila! Parbatti had phoned and told her that we were on our way, so she had rushed out of class to meet the bus. She knew Parbatti was bringing presents and money from us, and from Sue, when she visited her friend in a day or two, and Susila wanted to thank us.

She had grown up over the past two years and had become a very lovely young lady. We were thrilled to see her again, albeit for only a minute, and with the bus window between us!

The new passengers got on, the bus door rattled closed again, and in no time at all we were ready to leave.

Susila stood waving after the bus as it pulled away, in much the same way as her best friend Parbatti had done earlier. We smiled, remembering the pair of them four years ago at the little school in the mountains. They had once spent a full half hour hiding high up in a tree in the forest, while the rest of the class searched for them, and Tod and I panicked! Our games of 'Hide and Seek' were much more closely regulated after that!

I would like to take this opportunity to thank all those of you, too many to name, who contributed in any way to the vast pile of goodies which we took to Salle for the villagers and children. Thanks also to those who gave us money to distribute there.

The fact that people who didn't know them, who lived thousands of miles away in very different circumstances, had thought of them, and had sent them gifts, amazed and touched those wonderful villagers.

Your generosity was greatly appreciated.

CHAPTER NINE

Half way through the journey back to Kathmandu the bus stopped in a small village for a thirty minute break. Most of the passengers got off to stretch their legs and get something to eat. Tod and I remained on board, glad that the rough, bouncing, stuttering movement of the bus and accompanying roar and screech of the engine had ceased for a moment.

I glanced out the window, across the hard clay road at the uneven row of low wooden buildings on the other side, and caught sight of a movement on the ground outside one of them.

A man had just slaughtered a goat there, and was attempting to catch the blood spraying from the rough gash in the animal's throat in a plastic bowl. The goat was writhing on the ground, its legs stretched straight out, ready to carry it away from that dark place, and from that awful, uncaring, lonely destiny. But unable to flee it remained there; there amongst the sea of garbage, its warm blood spattering the filthy old plastic bags, ripped and discarded papers, and its killer's hands and trousers. Passers-by passed by with hardly a second glance.

Kalyani came running up the bus aisle as fast as she could,

"Tod! Fiona!" she shouted, "It's here! My Visa has arrived!" and she positively beamed at us. We had never seen her so excited. She had just taken a phone call telling her that her Visa for Australia was ready and waiting for her in Kathmandu!

So it was really going to happen. Kalyani was going to live in Australia.

Back in Kathmandu the next day she rang us at the hotel,

"I will come to have lunch with you," she told us, "And then I must go to buy my plane ticket!" she was so excited she could hardly speak!

We had lunch together at the hotel, sitting in the courtyard in the shade of the spreading tree, laughing, chatting and enjoying Kalyani's company for what could have been the last time. We didn't know whether it would be or not, and neither did she. But we were happy for her – why would we not have been,

"I will come to see you again tomorrow morning," she told us as she stood up to leave, "and I will tell you then when my plane goes."

We walked to the hotel gates with her, trying to smile, trying not to let her see how selfishly sad we were,

"See you tomorrow," she said and hugged us both, smiling up into our faces.

We watched her walk away down the short side road. She stopped at the end and looked back at us. Our Little Ant. Our friend.

She called, "Bye bye!" and waved. We waved back, and she disappeared round the corner onto the main street and was lost to our view. Our Little Ant. Our friend.

That evening Kalyani phoned us to say she had managed to get a flight to Australia leaving at eleven o'clock that very night. She was in a taxi on her way to the airport then. We wished her a safe journey and said goodbye as enthusiastically as we could.

We have neither seen her, nor spoken to her since, although happily we have maintained email contact.

Kalyani is happy in Australia. We hope to visit her there.

CHAPTER TEN

Chitwan, a tropical monsoon region in the south of Nepal, is situated along the Indian border. In contrast to the ultra-high, rugged and mountainous north of the country Chitwan is mostly flat, with vast flat floored valleys, and jungle areas criss crossed by a number of rivers.

It is probably best known for its National Park, a World Heritage Site, which attracts foreign tourists, who come to bask in the considerable heat and humidity of the jungle, and stare at the crocs, rhinos, and snooty camels who live there. I have never crossed the path of a camel who has not given me a haughty glare, so I do not feel that this is an unduly unfair observation.

But our friend Karma now also lives in Chitwan, although she and her husband are newcomers to that area.

Two months before we arrived back in Nepal this time they relocated from Kathmandu to Chitwan when they were offered the opportunity of supervising the opening of, and then running, a new brick making factory.

We met Karma in 2009 when we decided to visit Tibet. Luckily for us the Nepal-Tibet border had just opened and tourists were, if not exactly welcomed with open arms in that country, at least able to enter it with organised tours.

Karma worked in a tourist agency in Kathmandu, and she booked our trip to Tibet. The agency is across the road from the hotel we always stay in, so we saw quite a lot of Karma, and became very fond of her.

She is of Tibetan descent and we were impressed by her professionalism, her excellent English, and her wonderful, dry sense of humour. Nothing was too much trouble for her as far as we were concerned, and she became our own fairy godmother in Kathmandu.

One day, completely out of the blue, she said to us, "Have you ever tried Tibetan medication?"

"No," we said, wondering where this line of questioning was going,

"You should try it!" Karma said enthusiastically, "It is *very* good!"

"Oh; ok," we said, nodding politely, wondering if maybe we looked particularly ill that day. Had she spotted something wrong with us? Some awful disease we'd just caught? Did she know something that we didn't? We looked at each other. Was that a bit of a rash on Tod's neck?

"I will make an appointment for you," Karma said briskly, and wasting no time she picked up the phone, "the Tibetan doctors in Kathmandu are very good," she said, and proceeded to dial a number,

"But.....well.... umm.... *Why* would we need to visit a Tibetan doctor?" I asked timidly, rather afraid of what the answer to that question might be, "Umm....What sort of illness do they treat?"

"Everything!" Karma said, looking at me as if I was mad to even ask the question, "So," she said, looking us up and down, "what is wrong with you? What would you like the doctor to cure?"

"Ah, well...." I looked beseechingly at Tod. He was grinning. No help there then.

"What about a general help for your health?" Karma asked,

"Ah, yes; you mean a tonic?" I said helpfully, feeling relieved that we were not going to be forced to try something more exotic or outlandish.

Karma said something in Nepali into the phone, put it down and said,

"Ok, three o'clock tomorrow. I will take you."

So there we were; that was it. Our appointment was booked in the blink of an eye, whether we liked it or not!

Karma is probably in early middle age; a lovely looking lady with long dark hair and a beautiful complexion. She is certainly the most organised and efficient person in Kathmandu. Being taken under her wing meant that *we* got organised too. Hence the mysterious Tibetan medical appointment!

Karma was waiting for us outside the agency at exactly 3pm the next day. She was thrilled to be able to take us to the Pharmacy as she called it, and told us all about it as we walked there together through the noisy, bustling, colourful back streets of Kathmandu.

It seemed that the Pharmacy had been open for about thirty years, and the doctor and staff were all Tibetan. It was very popular, and always very busy. The only reason we had secured an appointment so quickly was because Karma had told them we were foreign, and would be returning home soon.

We walked for about fifteen minutes through narrow streets thronged with all manner of humanity, avoiding rickshaws, bicycles, cows, piles of rubble, and stepping over goods and food laid out on the ground for sale.

Then we turned off the road and onto a much smaller track lined on either side with high walls made from baked clay bricks. The afternoon sun reflected off the walls, and turned the narrow track into an airless oven. We puffed and panted along it (well, *I* did) for three or four minutes until we reached an archway in the wall on the left. Through it we could see a mass of trees and green vegetation, and as we stepped through the arch into the garden a wave of wonderfully cool, fresh air met us.

Wow! The garden was not huge, but it contained a number of exotic looking, glossy leaved trees of varying heights growing around a central, paved area. Their leaves threw shadows on the ground below them and provided shade from the heat of the sun.

Round this area, and enclosing it, were trellises made of wood, each standing six or eight feet tall, and completely covered with old, established climbing plants. They looked rather like clematis or honeysuckle, and the perfume from their numerous flowers hung delicately in the warm air.

There were simple wooden benches around the inside edges of the paved area, and half a dozen people were sitting there. They all looked up and smiled at us as we entered,

"This way," Karma said, and led us round the side of the sitting area towards a small, two storey white painted house. I had a brief impression of a house in need of repair, and of sturdy vines growing up the walls and hanging from the roof. Hansel and Gretel sprang to mind.

Karma climbed the couple of wooden steps up to the door and pushed it open. She spoke briefly to someone inside and then turned and beckoned to us to join her. We followed her in.

The room we entered was perhaps twelve feet square, and distinctly wooden. The old wooden floorboards creaked as we stepped on to them, and the dark wooden ceiling cast a dimness on the whole room. A high wooden counter along one side was laden with old books and ledgers, and behind it the wall was covered by wooden cupboards with glass doors, through which hundreds of bottles and containers of different shapes, sizes and colours were visible.

Perhaps twenty people were seated in silence on wooden benches around the room, and all eyes were disconcertingly upon us. I felt very vulnerable, and wanted to hide. A quick glance round confirmed that there was nowhere for us to sit. But a little problem like that would not faze Karma and she looked round, found a micro gap between two seated people, and asked them to move up. They duly did so, and so did the people next to them. Hey presto, a gap large enough for Tod, Karma and me to squeeze into magically opened up.

We smiled our thanks as we parked ourselves, with me sitting between Karma and Tod, and everyone smiled back at us. The room was perfectly quiet, no one spoke. I suppose the scene was much like a doctor's waiting room anywhere in the UK.

I discreetly examined our fellow bench sitters, and realised that perhaps 90% of them were Tibetan, or of Tibetan extract. Nothing odd there; after all, this *was* a Tibetan Pharmacy.

We were sitting opposite the wooden counter and I now saw that there were two women standing behind it, filling bottles with tablets, and writing in a ledger. They also appeared to be Tibetan, and were wearing long white coats, as befitted pharmacists anywhere in the world.

Karma whispered something to me, something unconnected to the Pharmacy, and I whispered back. We carried on our low level, mumbled conversation for a short time, and then Tod nudged me,

"You're getting the evil eye," he said, grinning and indicating one of the pharmacists who was positively glaring at Karma and me.

Oh dear, talking was obviously frowned upon in the waiting room, so we sat in contrite silence.

Not long after, the door to the doctor's room opened and a very small, very elderly woman came out. She was smiling broadly as she waved goodbye to the pharmacists and walked across the room to the exit. She appeared to be in rude health and full of energy, and her gait could certainly have been mistaken for that of a much younger woman. Karma looked at me and said quietly,

"You see Fiona; Tibetan medicine is good for all kinds of things. She looks very healthy!"

I had to agree. She certainly did.

It was pleasantly cool in the waiting room, and the atmosphere of calm quiet was very soothing. I closed my eyes. The only sounds were of tablets of some kind bouncing around as they were measured into bottles, and the crackling of paper as pages were turned in the ledgers,

"Fiona! Look!" Karma said softly, nudging me in the ribs, and I opened my eyes and glanced across at the man who had just come out of the doctor's surgery. He was obviously Tibetan, and rather than have his long hair tied up, as most Tibetan men did, it fell in thick curls around his face and onto his shoulders. His long, grey hair was certainly the first thing you would notice about him,

"Yesterday," Karma whispered to me, leaning closer, her expression dead-pan, "yesterday he was bald! So you see; Tibetan medicine is really *very* good!"

I couldn't help it. I couldn't stifle the loud chuckle and instead, with my hand over my mouth, it emerged as a kind of high pitched screaming snort. I looked down, trying to regain my composure, aware of the weight of all those astonished eyes on me; aware that, try as I might, I just couldn't stop giggling.

But I wasn't alone in that! Tod had heard what Karma said, and *oh no*, so had the man on Karma's other side. He had obviously understood her wise crack because he too had begun to giggle.

I looked up, met Karma's eyes, and the two of us dissolved into fits of laughter, aided and abetted by Tod and our new giggling friend on the other side.

Oh dear. In no time at all just about everyone in the waiting room was grinning broadly, and one or two were even laughing. It spread like wildfire. I don't think anyone else had heard what Karma said, or understood her comment, but when faced with four giggling adults, who have obviously seen the funny side of something, it is very difficult not to smile yourself.

Except, that is, if you are a pharmacist in a long white coat, whose avowed duty it is to keep order and silence, maybe even decorum, in the waiting room.

She walked quickly round the side of the counter, glared at each of us in turn, and then simply pointed silently to the door. You could have heard a pin drop in the room.

In a scene reminiscent of a 1920s English classroom drama the four of us stood up and slunk over to the door like naughty schoolchildren. But we were still giggling. And as we sat down on the benches outside in the garden we laughed and laughed. We couldn't stop. Every time I looked at Karma I started again!

The couple of people who were still waiting outside for their appointments stared at us in surprise, and then began to smile. We were obviously infectious!

Oh dear, the shame of it. I could now add to my CV the fact that I had been thrown out of a Tibetan Pharmacy for rowdy behaviour.

We finally settled down a bit and the mirth subsided. Eventually the house door opened and one of the pharmacists leaned out and beckoned to our new friend. He stood up and went in, nodding pleasantly to us as he passed. We did wonder if we would find him an hour later sitting alone in a corner and writing one hundred lines – '*I must not laugh in the Tibetan Pharmacy*'.

Eventually our turn came, and Karma accompanied us back inside. Tod and I entered the Tibetan doctor's surgery together, wondering what on earth we were letting ourselves in for. But she – yes, a lady – could not have been nicer; and a more educated, cultured and thoroughly pleasant doctor one could not have hoped to meet. We chatted for quite a while about 'the situation' in Tibet, and answered her questions as best we could about life in England.

We felt a bit like frauds, and explained that we were not really ill at all! But she understood, smiled, and gave us a Tibetan tonic! Karma was thrilled,

"You will really feel good with that," she told us enthusiastically,

"Will it make our hair grow?" I asked her,

"Maybe!" she said, "We will see!"

Karma rang us at home in England shortly after she and her husband had started their new life in Chitwan. We asked her how they were settling in, how they were enjoying it,

"It is good here, yes, but very boring. There is nothing to do," she told us, "no television, no internet, nowhere to buy books, no newspapers, and the nearby village is only very small. The villagers there all go to bed at 6pm!"

"Why?" we asked,

"Because of the rhinos!" she said, and laughed.

Had I heard her right? Had she *really* said 'because of the rhinos'? Humm…. I wasn't sure laughter was entirely appropriate at that particular juncture, but hey, what do *I* know about rhinos? Maybe *they* have a sense of humour,

"They come out of the jungle at 6pm," Karma went on, "and eat the sugar cane!" and she laughed again.

Right oh. I like an animal with regular eating habits. Nicely predictable.

We rang Karma from Kathmandu on our return from Salle, after Kalyani had left for her new life in Australia. We were ready to travel down to Chitwan to visit Karma. She was excited, looking forward to seeing us again, and we of course were looking forward to spending time with her and her husband, and seeing the new brick making factory - well, *Tod* was. *I* was looking forward to seeing the regular 6pm rhino munch.

We intended to travel to Chitwan by bus,

"My friend from the travel agency will take you to the bus stop, and he will buy the tickets for you," Karma said,

"Oh no, really; please don't worry about that," we said, "*We'll* find the bus stop; *we'll* get the tickets,"

"The bus goes from a different place now Fiona, not from the bus station. It is much further," she said, "and please believe me; you will *not* be able to find the bus stop. And….It is not nice there, at that place."

"Well," we said doubtfully, "if you're sure….?"

"I'm sure," she said, and told us what time to meet her friend from the agency where she used to work.

We met Karma's friend the next day and travelled to the bus stop in a taxi with him. It was indeed a long way from where we were staying, but as usual we thoroughly enjoyed seeing parts of Kathmandu, that once grand, spacious and elegant city, that were new to us.

However, as we neared our destination the young man turned round in his seat next to the driver and said to us,

"We are nearly arrived, and we can try to find the bus. This place is not clean; I'm sorry. Karma did not want you to come here alone," and he shook his head as he turned back and stared out the taxi window.

It was indeed 'not clean'. In fact the whole area, as far as we could see, was simply awash with rubbish.

We stepped out of the taxi, and found ourselves standing on a very wide, very crowded boulevard. We were at an intersection which seemed to be formed by the junction of two or three other boulevards, at a point where a massive, old steel bridge spanned the road.

It was quite early in the day and the wide, flat area around us was completely jammed with cars which seemed to be going in every direction possible, as fast as possible, and with no sense of order, or safety. With no road markings or signals it was difficult anyway to see just where they *should* have been going.

A strong wind whipped dust, gravel and rubbish up into massive, swirling tornadoes that distributed huge piles of garbage across the road in wave after stinking wave. Old plastic bags, ripped and disintegrating, became caught round car and bicycle wheels, and rogue papers skidded across car windscreens, momentarily blocking clear vision.

The whole sorry scene took your breath away. We covered our faces as best we could, and tried not to breathe any of the grimy air in.

I couldn't see if it was a road or rail bridge that spanned the mayhem below it, but the rusty construction seemed somehow to encourage a funnel effect around it, and the wind absolutely whipped through its structure, blowing dust up into a cloud that obscured its lower stanchions.

The far side of the wide road was edged by a rough, vertical rock face, which looked to be about ten or twelve feet high. It was covered in shreds of different coloured paper and plastic bags which had been blown against it, and now could not escape the pressure of the strong wind which held them there. It looked strange, surreal, like something created by a street artist, or made especially for the Tate Modern.

Our side of the road was edged by a row of low, dilapidated wooden buildings, hardly less covered by airborne rubbish than the rock face opposite, and outside which masses of people, mostly men, milled around. They seemed to be doing deals, buying and selling, and bargaining over any number of goods. We saw money changing hands.

Karma's friend told us to keep our small rucksacks with us, and to watch our pockets. We understood. I didn't feel particularly safe, and the chokingly filthy wind only added to my discomfort. No wonder Karma had insisted on her friend looking after us there. He walked off to find the bus and buy our tickets, looking back over his shoulder as he went to make sure we were ok. I moved closer to Tod.

The bus, when it arrived, was a small one; an eighteen seater. Karma had actually spoken to the driver and told him to take care of us! He pointed to the two seats directly behind the driver's seat, and we clambered in, taking our rucksacks with us. Karma's friend paid the driver for our seats, refused to let us reimburse him, and waved us goodbye,

"Be careful," he said as he left, "Keep your bags with you and watch your pockets," and he waved goodbye again and got back in the taxi which had waited for him. It drove off, swerving through the chaotic traffic jam, horn hooting as it went. I felt very alone when I could no longer see it.

We stared out the window at the picture of bedlam on the road outside. There was really nothing to say, so we sat in silence waiting for the bus to get going.

But it was about two and a half hours late leaving, probably because it waited in vain for four missing passengers, who never did show up.

From Kathmandu to Chitwan it is about 110 miles, but actual distance is almost irrelevant in Nepal, it's *how long* the journey takes that matters, and you can never be sure just how long that will be. So we finally set off, looking forward to our trip, but hoping that it would take no more than the estimated eight hours.

A couple of hours into the journey Tod discovered an army of small, biting red ants clambering all over him and having a nibble here and there, so we gathered our belongings together and settled down on the vacant back seat for the rest of the trip, which as it turned out, was singularly uneventful.

Late afternoon found us bouncing along rough tracks that cut across flat, wide open expanses of land that were planted with sugar cane and banana plantations as far as the eye could see. We knew we had reached Chitwan.

The banana trees did not seem very tall, maybe twenty or so feet high, but they clustered and crammed together in their hundreds, and filled the horizons all around. Their long, thick and lusciously green leaves, which are characteristically cut and divided into fingers along one of their edges, waved gently together in the hot breeze, atop a myriad of pale brown, bald trunks.

The bananas were not yet ripe, and hung down from the centre of the trees together in tight, heavy green masses, originating from a hidden spot somewhere in amongst their large leaves. The bananas were all neatly aligned in rows, fitting together like Lego pieces, as if they had just been expertly packed, ready for the supermarket. Isn't Nature fascinating?

It was hot. The sun beat down and the land was parched. I didn't envy those villagers we could see working on the fields.

The bus drove through an occasional small village, along eye wateringly narrow tracks running between small, round, thatched houses with walls made of dry clay. There were bamboo enclosures outside, housing water buffalo and goats, and groups of chickens and geese ran everywhere through the thick, dry dust.

Enormous cracks had opened up across the track in places and, unable to circumnavigate them due to the proximity of the houses, the bus crashed and juddered through them, throwing us all around inside.

Time was moving on, and our progress was slow,

"I hope we get there before 6pm!" I said to Tod, "I don't fancy being a rhino's dessert!"

Silence,

"Six o'clock....... You know; rhino tea time," I said helpfully, grinning at him.

Tod does do rather a good line in withering glances, and this was one of his better ones. I felt rather hurt.

The bus took us into the middle of nowhere. We ploughed round bends, up sharp little hills, down gullies; we squeezed between houses, the thatch of their roofs brushing and scraping the bus windows....and suddenly there it was; the new brick factory. The bus stopped, and we realised we had arrived. There was a moment of absolute peace and quiet as the noise of the engine died away.

Karma came running over and pulled the bus door open. She had an instant of panic when she saw we were not sitting in the seats behind the driver, and started to berate the poor man, no doubt asking him where he'd misplaced us along the way!

"Karma!" we shouted, "We're here!" and we struggled as fast as we could along the narrow aisle to the bus door.

It was wonderful to see Karma and her husband again, and we all laughed and hugged, then walked together across a huge, flat expanse of dry, dusty land, with patches of brown, scorched grass here and there, to a long, white, single storey building on the far side of it. Our footsteps raised little puffs of red dust at each step, and our boots quickly took on a reddish hue. Only the tumbleweed was missing.

We climbed quite a high, man-made, grassy bank and reached a flat, dry clay area in front of the building. I noticed that the bank ran around the whole compound, making the large central area appear oddly sunken. There was a wooden table and chairs outside the building, and Karma, her husband, Tod and I sat down. The heat was dry and breath-taking, and after a moment Karma disappeared into the building and reappeared with cool lemonade for us all. It was very quiet.

The building we were sitting outside was new, and had been constructed at the same time as the brick factory in order to provide Karma and her husband with a spacious room to live in, an office to work from, and a spare room.

The other key workers in the new business had settled into rooms of their own too, further along the building.

The bus, which had stopped in the middle of the compound, now revved up its engine and moved off, the driver waving and shouting goodbye out the window as it went. It left a thick trail of red dust hanging in the still, hot air behind it.

We sat and looked with interest across the compound at the new factory opposite. I had never seen a brick factory close up. Eventually we all walked over to it, and Karma and her husband showed us round. There did not seem to be a great deal to see. A large hopper stood at one end of a conveyor belt, and there was a wide, open area used for drying the moulded bricks at the other.

The process was entirely automated, and would employ thirty workers when it was up and running. The whole factory area was covered by a high roof supported by tall columns, but there were no walls, thereby permitting what cooling breeze there was to blow through.

The brand new chimney and kilns had been constructed alongside the compound, and Karma showed us a series of little huts nearby, also brand new, which were for the itinerant workers to sleep in.

We walked slowly round as Karma pointed out various landmarks, and introduced us to the one or two other people we met along the way.

The land around the factory was perfectly flat as far as the eye could see. It rolled out in front of us, shimmering below a thick heat haze that made the crops of rice, potatoes, corn and sugar cane appear oddly to shiver and tremble through the hot air.

We walked round the back of the 'office' building and found a river meandering sluggishly behind the compound. It wasn't particularly wide, maybe one hundred feet at most, and its irregular twists and turns had cut deeply into the steep banks on one side, and spread out over a gentle slope on the other.

The river was only half full, but the marks high up on its banks testified to the fact that if we had visited in autumn or winter we would have seen a very different river; a faster moving, uninviting, and possibly dangerous river.

A group of small children were playing happily in the water. It appeared none too clean, although it might just have been stained by the reddish coloured soil that it ran through, making it appear dark and murky. But the children didn't mind. They were having a great time!

We smiled as we watched them messing around in the water in the way any group of children would do anywhere in the world, except.... *they* were playing with a water buffalo! They were splashing it, jumping on its back, and washing it down, and I swear that wonderful creature had a grin on its face.

Karma, never one to let the grass grow under her feet, had started to make good use of the considerable amount of spare land her company had bought around the brick factory.

She had dug a large pond behind the office building and stocked it with fish, with a view to providing some extra food for the workers. I was impressed, and amazed. Where on earth had she got the fish from?

"A man," she told me, "A man."

Right oh.

The pond was maybe twenty feet by ten, and certainly a good couple of feet deep. I suspect she had a bit of help to dig it. We sat down on the ground at the edge of the pond and looked around. It was wonderfully quiet and peaceful there. She had planted bushes at various points around, and a low fence marked out her vegetable garden, where potatoes, carrots, lettuce and beans were already growing. I remembered that we had sent her some seeds, and was glad to see that they had been put to good use.

A colony of frogs had moved in and made the pond and the surrounding area their home. They demonstrated just for us their amazing and amusing ability to run across the *surface* of the water. How cool is that! Frogs who can walk on water.

We watched them. They would stand immobile at the edge of the pond, looking serious and contemplating the water, obviously working out its depth. (Well, *I* think so). Then they would carefully raise a leg, foot pointing slightly outwards, and hold that position for a moment. Then, *wayhey!* They would set off at speed across the surface of the pond, each foot raised in turn and pointing outwards, forearms held slightly away from the body to retain their balance.

They looked just like cartoon figures of wobbly, little old men who had taken a wrong turn somewhere and found themselves shockingly standing on a pond.

Karma was very proud of the goats and chickens that ran around, and she showed us their newly built, safe sleeping quarters. But her piece de resistance was a newly acquired pair of pigs. They were magnificent, and she just loved them! (Three months down the line she didn't love them quite as much, as they had broken into her vegetable garden and eaten the lot!)

We had walked completely round the site, and now returned to the table and chairs, and sat down again. Evening was falling, bringing cooler air with it.

Six o'clock arrived, and I asked Karma where the rhinos were. She told us that the sugar cane plantation alongside the compound that the rhinos had particularly favoured had just been harvested, so they had moved on to another plantation, further away. Just our luck!

Karma's husband was pleased to see the back of them as he had come face to face with a rhino in the dark, only the previous week. And that's something you *really* don't want to do. He had discovered a latent and very useful ability to sprint!

Tod and I noticed a rather lovely large, white bird, standing alone on the grassy bank nearby. We thought it was a goose, but Karma assured us that it was, in fact, a swan.

The bird stood quietly, unmoving, on the grassy mound at the corner of the compound, beak raised, gazing into space,

"If you watch him he'll do yoga for you," Karma said, grinning,

"Really?" we said, "Yoga?"

"Yes!" she said, "Yoga!"

We watched; and he did.

Would you believe, the swan slowly raised one leg and stretched it out behind him, pink web and tiny nails neatly pointed downwards. Then he slowly stretched out his wing on the same side, until it was completely extended horizontally, each white feather clearly visible and neatly aligned.

He remained in that position, gazing intently upwards, beak pointing towards the sky, towards the sun, away from the hot, dry earth that held him back.

Oh boy! Oh wow! A yogic swan!

Karma's brick factory is fully automated. There is housing of sorts, water and a toilet for the workers, and Karma cooks two meals a day for them, every day.

After breakfast the next morning she took us across the river behind the compound to see round a neighbouring brick factory. This one is worked entirely by hand. There is no water supply provided for the workers, and no toilet available for them.

The temperature was already in the thirties (centigrade) at 9am as we walked across to the factory. It was a scorching, enervating heat; the kind of heat that makes every action an unpleasant effort.

All the work is done outside at this factory, and our initial misgivings grew into something akin to horror as we saw the conditions that existed there.

Bricks were laid out everywhere, over a huge area, as different family groups worked on them by hand in the searing heat. Small, undernourished ponies pulled primitive-looking carts, laden with bricks, from one place to another, struggling to get the heavy loads started, as their drivers used whips to urge them on.

We saw many children working there, many of them very young, and one as young as four years old.

A brisk, burning wind fanned brick dust over everyone, everywhere. The dust grabbed at the back of your throat making you retch and cough. We covered our mouths as best we could, grateful for the bottles of water Karma had insisted that we bring.

The workers and children had no masks, no facial protection, and several of the children had obvious eye infections. One or two of the adults seemed ill. They sat on the ground amongst piles of bricks, listless, suffering, watching us without expression.

We wanted to give money to those workers who seemed most in need, but Karma was very firm,

"I'm sorry," she said, "you can't. There are three hundred workers here, and if you give money to some, and not to others, it may cause a riot."

Protesting did no good. Our friend was sensibly adamant.

So we turned our backs on the men, women and children struggling to make a living out there amongst the sea of bricks, in the searing heat and merciless wind, with their rags and pieces of ripped plastic draped over sticks for their shade and shelter.

And we turned our backs on the little ponies who would never know any other life, and would keep on working faithfully until they dropped.

We walked slowly back across the river, weighed down by the anger of helpless guilt. Even the revelation that Karma was personally helping some of the families in that hellhole did nothing to alleviate our guilt.

Nothing could.

Life seemed suddenly a whole lot darker.

As well it should.

Later, Karma told us stories about the people who work with her in the new brick factory; about the area; and about the villagers from the nearby small, isolated community. We listened with interest,

"They live as if they are five hundred years in the past," she told us, nodding towards the small group of clay and thatch houses which were just visible through the heat haze, "The children do not go to school, and the men have three wives each."

Just the day before we arrived to visit Karma a villager in her sixties had been severely beaten up by her own family, and thrown out of her house onto the track outside, where a number of other villagers also beat her, to within an inch of her life.

Why? Because they said she was a witch.

A child from the village came running to fetch Karma and her husband, begging them to come and help the poor woman. They did, and carried her nearly two miles to a local 'hospital' where the woman received treatment. She was still there.

It was obvious that the woman would not be accepted back into the village, so Karma had given her money to enable her to travel to her daughter's village, quite some distance away. She would hopefully be able to settle there once she had recovered from her injuries.

The company which Karma works for paid to have a landline telephone installed at the factory. It was no simple matter, involving bringing the cable some miles along telegraph poles. When finally the installation was complete, and the last telegraph pole was securely upright, next to the compound, the phone line was tested and found to be working. Success.

The next day the telegraph pole had vanished without trace, leaving the cable broken and lying uselessly on the ground.

It wasn't long before the culprits were unmasked, as the villagers were discovered trying to chop up a long, wooden pole for firewood. But the damage was done. The telegraph pole could not be restored, and the company have since thought better of replacing it. They now rely on the unreliable mobile phone signal in order to keep in touch with the business.

A very pleasant, very elderly man came to say hello to us, and Karma introduced him as the factory 'security guard',

"He stays awake every night to watch the factory," Karma told us,

"What a shame that he has to do that," we said, "He should be enjoying his old age and relaxing, not working nights."

"Yes, it is sad," she said, "but he lived all his life in the village, and has five sons. He had a lot of land, and because he was old he gave the land to his sons, thinking they would care for him in his old age. But they threw him and his wife out – out of their house, out of the village. So now the couple are penniless and homeless. My company have employed him, so at least they can eat."

A pleasant young woman came over to speak to Karma, and was introduced to us as Bina. She was employed as a kitchen assistant, but Karma was training her to take over all the catering for the factory staff.

Most of Bina's face was completely covered by a scarf which she had wrapped around her head, and although only her eyes were visible she kept her head turned away from us as much as possible.

This is her story:

Two years earlier Bina was married and had two small children. She worked at the brick factory across the river. She was cooking a meal for her husband one evening on an oil pumped cooker when it exploded, and covered her in burning oil. Her husband had been drinking and was asleep. Her terrified screams eventually woke him, and thinking only to put out the flames, he threw water over her. The water hit the burning oil and caused a fireball, which severely burned Bina's face and upper body.

She spent five or six months in hospital, and had several operations on her face, but returned home eventually with terrible facial scarring. The consequences of this dreadful accident were devastating.

Very few people would even look at her, let alone speak to her. The brick factory where she had worked refused to take her back because of her scars, and her husband left her soon after for another woman, cutting off all contact, and financial support, for Bina and her children.

Her brother, who lives in another part of Nepal, refused to see her or have anything to do with her, but Bina's sister, who lives abroad, sent her money so she could at least feed her children.

Karma heard about Bina's plight and spoke to her employers. Karma's company not only employs Bina now, but they pay for her children's education too.

However, although certain aspects of her life have improved, Bina's future remains bleak. The ignorance which has caused her so much heartache dictates that she will never again be able to show her face in public, for fear of violent repercussions.

Our time with Karma and her husband went too quickly.

The return bus trip left at 3am the following day, and we staggered, bleary eyed, back onto the same bus, with the same driver who had brought us to Chitwan. We sat on the back seat for what turned out to be a pretty uneventful journey back to Kathmandu.

We speak to Karma regularly. She has replanted her vegetable garden.

CHAPTER ELEVEN

Towards the end of 2010 on a cold, damp, winter's day in the north of England, an attractive, glossy magazine dropped through the letter box of our front door.

We were busy at that time; both of us completely consumed with a number of different projects, and the magazine lay untouched and unopened on the kitchen counter for several days.

Eventually Tod picked it up and sat down in the conservatory to flick through it. I followed him in, and sat down myself to read a newspaper.

Driving rain hammered down on the roof, falling so heavily that it almost obliterated the usually pleasant view of the garden outside. It reminded us just how bleak an English winter can be, if indeed we needed reminding.

I sighed and glanced across at Tod. The photo on the front cover of the magazine caught my attention. I craned my neck to see it better, just as Tod closed the mag and himself stared at the photo.

He looked over at me, and back at the photo. Oh dear; I recognised that look. It usually presaged some kind of project, and *that* frequently involved some dire physical effort on *my* part!

The noise of the rain bouncing on the roof seemed suddenly to diminish, to fade into the background, and I got up and went over to sit by him.

Together we looked closely at the photo of probably the most amazing, the most beautiful Buddhist Temple we had ever seen.

It was perched, literally, on the side of a mountain, hanging on to the rock, above a sheer drop of thousands of feet, clinging by some Heaven-sent miracle to bare rock and thin air.

Stunning building; absolutely stunning location.

"Where is it?" Tod asked, and I just *knew* that he didn't really *care* where it was, he just wanted to *go* there; he just wanted to climb up to it through the clouds, and to see the world from its perspective. Tod was smitten,

"Strangely, it doesn't say where it is," I told him, "I'll email the mag and find out."

So that was it. That remarkable, spine-tingling, soul-touching Buddhist Temple was added to our long list of 'things to do when we have the time', or in *my* case, when I have the energy!

The answer to my email enquiry told me that the Temple was called 'Tiger's Nest' and it was located high in the Himalayas, in Bhutan.

Taktsang Palphug Monastery, or Tiger's Nest as it is more commonly known, is situated at an altitude of 10,000ft in the tiny country of Bhutan which, oddly enough, is very near Nepal. In fact only the small Indian state of Sikkim, located on Bhutan's western border, stands between the two countries. If you are a particularly gifted crow, able to fly straight and true between Kathmandu and Bhutan's capital city Thimphu, the journey will not take you long, for the distance is only two hundred and sixty five miles.

But at that time we knew next to nothing about the country of Bhutan, except this:

In 2009, while we were living and teaching English in the remote village of Salle in the Everest Region of Nepal, we spent a lot of time with Kalyani, who was then the young village school headmistress.

As I'm sure I've mentioned many times before, laughter was never very far away when the three of us were together. Kalyani has a wicked, dry sense of humour, and a tendency to see the funny side of just about any situation, much as *we* do.

Three teachers, all young women, were employed at the village school. A fourth teacher joined the staff while we were there. He was a young man from Bhutan, who came with a very sad story.

He and his family were refugees now living in Kathmandu, following a landslip in Bhutan which had completely destroyed the family house and the land which they had owned.

The family then relocated to Nepal, and he got the job as a teacher in the village school in Salle.

Regrettably, he was a somewhat gauche and socially rather difficult young man who did not endear himself to the elders and villagers of Salle at the very beginning of his association with them, by demanding four sacks of rice for his monthly salary, rather than the accepted three. Village hackles rose; rice was hard to come by up there in the mountains,

"How can he eat so much?" Kalyani said, "What is he *doing* with it?"

Her aggrieved tone made us laugh, and we had some fun speculating on what the new teacher from Bhutan might be doing with the extra sack of rice.

But, unfortunately for the young man, something unknown that he regularly ate or drank in the village did not agree with him, and in just a very short time he seemed to be constantly suffering from an upset stomach.

It may have been the food, maybe even the rice, or it may perhaps have been the water. Nobody knew. So he moved to Lohrimani, the next village, and lodged with a family there. But he found no respite in his new situation, and his stomach problems continued, making life increasingly difficult for him.

As if his bad stomach were not enough to contend with, he was also not happy in his new job. Amongst other things, he did not like the teaching methods in use in the village school, and he also did not get along with the other teachers who, finding him to be rude, critical and unsympathetic, eventually avoided him as much as possible.

His route to the village school from Lohrimani passed by the house we were staying in, and he took to waiting for us outside in the mornings, and walking with us. Of course we collected Kalyani on the way, so that meant the four of us would have to walk together.

It was not a happy troupe! The young man complained loudly and constantly, in both Nepali and in English, about his health, about the weather, about the job, and managed to get on Kalyani's nerves in a big way,

"How is your stomach today?" she'd ask him politely, and he would moan and groan, and provide far too much information; far too many details for our comfort!

Tod and I would fall about laughing just watching Kalyani trying to remain polite with the poor chap. It eventually reached the point when Tod, Kalyani and I would hide in the mornings, and wait for him to walk past the house, before we set off to school at a safe distance behind him.

Early on Tod had named the unfortunate young man 'Bubbly Bum' for obvious reasons, and Kalyani just loved the sound of that nickname. She always pronounced it Bu-buh-lee – Bum.

I am ashamed to tell you that the three of us were often to be seen, and heard, walking along one mountain track or another, singing loudly:

"Bubbly Bum, Bubbly Bum; here comes Bubbly Bum!"
Oh dear.

I hasten to add that the young man never knew we had given him a nickname!

But he could not settle in Salle or in Lohrimani and, disillusioned with life up in the mountains of the Everest Region, he eventually moved back to Kathmandu.

Bhutan is a tiny, remote country, nestled in the rugged folds of the Himalayas between big brother India on its southern, eastern and western borders, and China on its northern border. It has a population of about 750,000.

The spectacular natural beauty of Bhutan ranges from subtropical plains in the south of the country, to the Himalayan heights in the north. The vast majority of Bhutan is thickly forested and much of it is unexplored; for sure Yeti and tigers roam the high, remote, untouched regions, hunting their prey in the safety and seclusion of a country which vows to forever retain a minimum of 60% forest cover throughout.

Bhutan was almost completely cut off from the rest of the world for centuries, unwilling to risk the pollution of foreign influence on its way of life, but its borders opened just a crack in the 1970s, to allow a small number of tourists to enter each year, though only with certain state approved, organised groups.

In 2008 Bhutan moved from being an Absolute Monarchy to a system of Constitutional Monarchy, within a two party Parliamentary democracy. Both political parties are solidly pro Monarchy, and the King and Royal Family are much loved, and remain highly influential in Bhutan today.

Bhutan guards its traditions fiercely, and national dress is compulsory for the population – knee length wrap arounds for men, and ankle length dresses for women.

Buddhism is the state religion, with Hinduism being the second largest religious group in the country.

The wonderfully evocative term 'Gross National Happiness', invented in 1972 by Bhutan's fourth King, denotes the balance between spiritual and material life. GNH has become an integral measure of the wellbeing of the people of Bhutan, and the concept has attracted worldwide interest.

In 2006 'Business Week' published information based on a global survey, and rated the Bhutanese people the "Happiest in Asia", and the "Eighth happiest in the world".

We were really excited about our forthcoming trip to Bhutan, and particularly about visiting Tiger's Nest. I spent hours staring at pictures of that magical monastery on the internet, marvelling at its beauty, and panicking that I may not be able to climb up to it. After all, it was up a Himalayan *cliff* for goodness sake!

I placed my hope in the horses. Apparently you could ask a handy horse if it would be willing to carry you one third of the way up to Tiger's Nest. Oh wow! Yes please!

I trawled the internet looking for the Bhutanese equine words for 'Would you please carry me up the mountain?' and hoped that my pronunciation would be acceptable to equine ears.

We flew from Kathmandu to Paro airport, in the west of Bhutan, early one bright, warm morning.

Now, I don't consider myself to be a particularly sneaky kind of person, but I do sometimes work on a 'need to know' basis with Tod, particularly where information regarding our adventures is concerned. It makes life a little easier, and enables me to avoid having to try to find answers to any awkward questions.

This was indeed one of those times when I felt sure that a certain amount of, shall we say, *economy* with the truth was called for.

So, I hadn't mentioned to my safety conscious better half that the runway at Paro airport would probably fit pretty easily into our back garden. Actually, it is a whole 6,500ft long, or 1,980 meters, which may *sound* long, but try landing a plane on it, or rather, try *stopping* a plane on it *after* landing!

I had read a quote somewhere on the internet attributed to 'Boeing' (who should know a thing or two about flying planes) stating that Paro Airport is one of the world's most *difficult* for take offs and landings.

Oh yeah! Difficult? *Difficult?*

Right oh.

And I obviously hadn't mentioned to Tod that there are only a small number of pilots (eight, actually, as of 2012) who are trained and competent to *land* on said runway.

Oh, and add to that the fact that the approach to the runway is along a flat floored valley, winding between Himalayan peaks reaching 18,000ft, and around which squally, unpredictable winds regularly race and roar. The steep, rocky walls of the valley are just about wide enough apart for a plane to fit between them, wing tip to wing tip, practically brushing the mountains on either side.

And don't let's forget the right angled bend at the end of the valley; a bend which needs to be negotiated pretty sharpish, before the runway even trundles into view.

And *then* there's the river! Yes! The river that winds along the valley floor and crosses it just *in front of* the landing strip!

So, actually dropping onto this landing strip would seem to be fraught with all kinds of problems – narrow valley, reduced visibility, unpredictable winds, sharp bend, river in the way. But, having managed by some miracle to *land* on the strip, don't be tempted to sit back and feel smug. You are hurtling along, eating runway at the speed of light. 6,500 feet of landing strip will not take long to digest, and guess what…. 6,600 feet along it you will encounter a mountain. Yes indeedy, a mountain. A Himalayan mountain.

The landing strip at Paro airport has been squeezed into probably the only flat piece of land around, and there are not many of them up there in the Himalayas.

God bless those eight pilots.

Actually, I didn't mention *any* of that to *anyone*, and certainly not to my friend Maria, who's a bit too fond of saying, "What are you getting poor Tod into now?" in an accusatory kind of way. Mind you, that *was* after I'd sent him up for a ride in a micro-light for his birthday present.

So, off we went from Kathmandu in a plane which surprised me by its size. I had expected it to be small; really small; small enough to squeeze along the valley up to Paro airport, and small enough to stop before it ran off the end of the landing strip, the landing strip that measures a meagre 6,500ft.

But instead we were in a much bigger plane than I would have selected myself, and I have to admit to feeling just a bit nervous as we boarded.

Good oh. Nothing like a bit of adrenaline to focus the mind and sharpen the senses.

It was a short and uneventful flight, except that we flew straight past Everest. But by the time the pilot had told us all to, "Look to your left" there was nothing to see except cloud and snow-capped peaks. The world's highest mountain, and we missed it.

As we began the descent towards Paro airport a noticeable hush fell upon the previously yappy passengers. I wondered how many of them knew that we were headed for arguably one of the ten most 'difficult' airstrips to land or take off from in the world.

I glanced out the window and saw mountain, just outside, heart stoppingly near. Stupidly I looked over at the window across the aisle and saw mountain, just outside, heart stoppingly near.

I reached out and took Tod's hand,

"Is there something you haven't told me?" he asked. No flies on him then,

"Just a bit of stuff I didn't mention. Tell you later," I said, hoping there *would* be a 'later'.

The landing was, without doubt, an experience I would have to rate as probably the most nerve wracking of my life.

The sudden rush and squeal of brakes as the plane struggled to stop on the runway sent a wave of anxious fidgeting sweeping through the passengers, but it was quickly replaced by relieved laughter, and a smattering of applause, as we came to a full stop,

"That was fun," I said. Tod stared at me with rather an odd expression on his face, and I suddenly realised that he was probably the only passenger who hadn't known what kind of scary landing to expect. I wondered for a moment if that was a good thing or a bad thing.

We got off. I handed the camera to Tod, and he took it from me in silence. He didn't ask me why he needed the camera. It was obvious. You don't often see a plane standing right at the very end of a runway, next to a mountain. He walked across to join the other passengers who were all taking photos. I followed him,

"I may have been just a bit economical with some details about the flight, and....you know.... the landing in particular," I told him, smiling to try to soften the blow.

He ignored me, and took several photos in silence.

Oh dear.

CHAPTER TWELVE

Our first impression of Bhutan was that it is neat, clean, and ordered, with magnificent scenery of towering, forested mountains and deep, green and fertile valleys. It is a picture of neatly cared for remoteness, of general appreciation and nurture of nature and eco systems, and of regulated and careful human progress.

Our guides told us that the whole country teemed with wildlife, and we found that easy to believe.

But it is very expensive to visit Bhutan, and any would be tourist must part with $250 US per day (as of 2013), although that *does* include hotels, transport and tourist attractions. There is no way round it, and coupled with the necessary Visas, it is an often prohibitive condition of entry to the country.

We planned to stay only two days. After all, our prime reason for being there at all was to visit Tiger's Nest, which we were due to do on our last day there.

Our two young and pleasant Bhutanese guides, who had collected us at the airport, arrived at the hotel to pick us up the next day exactly on time. We, unfortunately and embarrassingly, were exactly fifteen minutes late, due entirely to that rogue quarter of an hour which had tricked us yet again, and managed to follow us from Nepal. What *is* going on?

The two lads just laughed. In the land of Gross National Happiness what's fifteen minutes between friends?

In many ways they were not so very different to a couple of young lads you might find anywhere in Europe or the USA. They wanted to discuss music, films, and motorbikes. They were thrilled to learn that Tod builds motor trikes, and wanted to know all about them. They had their beloved mobile phones glued to their hands, used the internet, and asked us plenty of questions about life in the

UK. The most obvious difference, I suppose, was the fact that these two lads, and all of their peers, wore Bhutanese national dress, and wore it with pride.

We spent the day driving around with them, visiting a number of attractions, beginning with the world's largest sitting Buddha.

'Impressive' would only just *begin* to describe the enormous, jaw dropping 169ft (51.5 metres) tall statue of Shakyamuni Buddha, which is made entirely of bronze gilded with gold. The site at which the statue is located, Kuenselphodrang Nature Park, high in the mountains just outside the southern approach to Thimphu, was not finished, and most of the area looked rather like a building site. But the Buddha was in place atop a hill, and gazed serenely down upon the vista of the Thimphu valley, where clusters of new, characteristically distinctive white and brown buildings were beginning to encroach on the remaining green slopes of the valley walls. Every new building in Bhutan must be created in the traditional style, with Buddhist paintings and motifs on them.

Even from that altitude we could see the development that was going on in and around Thimphu, a city of roughly 105,000 inhabitants, which only became the capital of Bhutan in 1961.

The colossal statue positively glowed and glinted in the bright morning sunshine, sending out little sparkles of reflected light, and dwarfing everyone and everything around it.

Our guides explained that the statue, known as Buddha Dordenma, fulfils an ancient prophecy, and will bestow blessings, peace and happiness on the whole world.

Its base will be a huge meditation centre, and the Buddha itself will eventually house 100,000 small Buddha statues, each made of bronze and gilded in gold.

Tod and I stood in the middle of the vast open area in front of the statue, staring up at it, mesmerised. There is nothing quite like a massive religious statue to underline the insignificance of a human, and at that moment we felt like a pair of dumb struck ants.

No more than half a dozen other sightseers walked slowly around, staring up at the Buddha, taking photos and, oddly, speaking in whispers. The statue's influence was such that the whole area was peaceful, calm, and somehow other worldly.

Suddenly we heard,

"Hello! Hello!" and looked round to see who was shouting in this huge, almost silent area. A young man, wearing western clothes, was running towards us. We looked at each other,

"Who's that?" I asked,

"Dunno," Tod said, "Maybe he thinks we're someone else."

But the young man *didn't* think we were someone else. He hadn't made a mistake. He had recognised Tod from Kathmandu airport!

As we sat waiting in Kathmandu for our flight to Bhutan we noticed that one of the airport information boards was displaying incorrect data, and thereby causing no end of problems for would be passengers. We started to point the errors out to traveller after traveller, making sure they knew that the flight times and numbers they were looking at were wrong. We practically got ourselves jobs at the airport.

One very pleasant young man was particularly grateful to us, and shook Tod's hand. He told us he was from South Korea, but that was really just about as far as we got because he spoke very little English, and we spoke no South Korean at all!

And now here he was, running towards us in the shadow of the world's largest sitting Buddha! He had recognised Tod from afar! I can't think why.

101

He and Tod hugged, and we all laughed at the happenstance that found us there together. I wish we could have communicated a bit better, but after a few moments we said goodbye, and went our separate ways.

Did you know that the Takin is the National Animal of Bhutan?
Neither did we.
'What *is* a Takin?' I hear you ask, as indeed *we* did, when our guides told us we were going to see some,
"They live in a special Reserve near Thimphu," they said, "The Takin do not want to be completely wild,"
"Sorry?" I said, "What do you mean....'they don't want to be completely wild'?" That was a very odd statement, and one which I felt needed clarifying. Is there an animal anywhere on the planet that, given the chance, would not *prefer* to be wild? Well, maybe,
"You see, in the 1980s our King felt that it was not correct, not right, for the National Animal of Bhutan, a Buddhist country, to be kept as a prisoner in a Reserve. So he ordered the Takin to be set free," our guide told us, "But they didn't want to go away; so they stayed."
Apparently, when the Takin were liberated from the small Reserve they lived in in the 1980s, no arrangements or preparations at all were made for the creatures' new life in the wild. The gate was simply opened, and they were allowed to walk out, which of course they eventually did.
But obviously the poor Takin didn't know where to go, or what to do, and ended up wandering the streets of Thimphu for several weeks looking for food.
A new, bigger Reserve was subsequently prepared for them, with access from it to high, mountain areas, and a plentiful food supply. They now live happily there.
So I suppose our guide was right, in a sense, to say that the Takin didn't want to be completely free; for at the time,

without access to a food supply, or the correct habitat, they were not able to make that choice and 'revert' to the wild.

These days Takin can be found living wild in the mountains of North West and North East Bhutan, in North East India, Western China, and Tibet. They manage best in rugged, mountain terrain at above 4,000ft., and they seem to be able to eat most greenery, but prefer a diet of bamboo.

So, we bade farewell to the Buddha Dordenma, that mind boggling, colossal statue, and off we went to the Takin Reserve in the mountains on the other side of the city of Thimphu.

We were curious to see what the Takin looked like, given that our guides just giggled and raised their eyebrows when we asked about them,

"They are sort of a mix of different animals; a bit of this and a little bit of that," they said, and dissolved into giggles again.

Right oh. We'll wait, we said, and see for ourselves. I like a good mystery.

We drove back through Thimphu again, gaining a fleeting impression of clean streets, clean buildings, grassy parks and….a massive amount of ongoing building development.

The Motithang Takin Reserve is located towards the north west of Thimphu. It is actually being gradually absorbed into the city, as development eats away at the open spaces around it. We parked in the small car park, next to the only other car there, and followed our guides up along a rough, steep path that the passage of many feet had cut deeply down into the dry clay soil. It was very quiet.

The path wound past fragrant conifer trees, their shed needles piled in dry drifts around the base of their trunks, and across small, open patches of grassland. We walked past a couple of wooden chalet-type huts, with a young girl sitting on the ground outside one of them, surrounded by scarves and other locally made items which were for sale.

We walked on, and a chain link fence appeared on our right, alongside the path,

"The Takin are behind the fence," our guide told us, smiling.

We stopped and stared through at conifer trees, dry tangled undergrowth, and patches of grass dappled by sunlight. No Takin; no movement,

"Where are they?" I asked,

"Maybe further on," the guide said, and walked ahead,

"Do you think they're so small we can't see them?" I said to Tod. He ignored me. I'm used to it.

We walked on in expectant silence, staring through the fence as we went, and then,

"There they are," Tod said quietly, pointing to a mound some way off between the trees,

"That's just a mound; soil or something," I said,

"Put your glasses on," he said. I felt that comment was uncalled for, especially as I *was* wearing my glasses,

"Oh wow!" I breathed, as the 'mound' stood up, and slowly made its way towards us. I had never seen anything like it, "Look at that!" I squeaked, "It's wonderful; what an amazing creature!"

"Certainly different," Tod said, and we found ourselves giggling rather like our guides had done.

The Takin looks, from the front, rather like a moose or reindeer, with a longish, moose-like face and big dark eyes. They have short horns that run alongside the face and curve at the ends. Their coats are usually dark brown or golden, and they stand about fifty inches high.

The humped shoulders seem to be about right for a moose, and the legs are rather short and muscular. But then it's all downhill towards the tail!

I really don't wish to be rude or hurtful to the poor Takin, but in fact you'd swear that it was two different animals stuck together. Something like Dr Dolittle's Pushmi-pullyu!

It is indeed a bizarre looking, though incredibly endearing creature, possessing a delightfully calm and peaceful nature.

The Takin are not naturally particularly lively apparently, and tend to rouse themselves for breakfast and tea, but spend the rest of their time relaxing. I know quite a few people like that.

The guide told us that the couple of Takin we could see in the Reserve were, sadly, seriously overweight, due to all kinds of unsuitable food being thrown to them by tourists, in defiance of the 'Please Do Not Feed' notices.

We stood for ages watching those incredible animals, and wondering at their provenance! The Takin will make you giggle.

On our way back down to the car we stopped to read the notice board that told us why the Takin had been chosen as the National Animal of Bhutan. It is a wonderful story, as befits a wonderful animal:

When the 15th century Tibetan holy man, Drukpa Kunley, visited Bhutan, he spoke to large gatherings of local people. Drukpa Kunley is said to have been severely unconventional, to say the least, and was widely known as the Divine Madman.

The people asked him to perform a miracle, and he agreed to do so, but only after he had eaten lunch, for which he demanded a whole cow, and a whole goat.

The holy man scoffed the lot; the entire cow and the entire goat. All that was left was a pile of bones.

Mindful that he had promised his audience a miracle he raised the cow's bones up, until it was standing with everything in the right order, and then he stuck the goat's head onto it.

He commanded this 'new' animal to come alive, which it did. It then ran to the meadow and began to graze.

How cool is that!

CHAPTER THIRTEEN

The next morning we drove to the base of Tiger's Nest Mountain and parked in a gravelled area completely enclosed by thick forest. The silence was overwhelming, all consuming, as if the forest had simply absorbed all trace of sound, and eaten any stray noises.

We couldn't see the Monastery. The mountains are mostly thickly wooded, right up to their summits, and from where we stood we couldn't see more than a few yards through the trees in front of us,

"Follow the path," our guides told us, "We will see you up there," and they trotted off into the forest and were quickly lost to view.

We set off after them, walking uphill through the stonily silent forest, across an upward sloping grassy clearing that suddenly appeared in front of us, and back into the forest again, as the slope became increasingly steeper.

Suddenly,

"There they are!" Tod said, pointing to a completely silent group of thirty or so horses standing together amongst the trees. We had almost walked past without noticing them. Not a single snort, not a jingle from reins, not a stamp from a hoof. How odd.

They were small, sturdy creatures, with thick brown and white coats and long manes, each wearing a colourful blanket as a saddle. I noticed how big their eyes were, how long the curving lashes. I noticed because they were all looking over in our direction. Every one of them. They almost seemed to be holding their breath, wondering which human was going to ask for their help to reach Tiger's Nest.

I already knew that I would be able to ask a horse, and I *do* mean 'ask', if he/she would agree to carry me a third of the way up to Tiger's Nest. A third of the way up was all that was allowed in consideration of the horses' health and wellbeing. And it would also be a one way journey, because it was too dangerous for the horses to bring passengers back down the mountain – the track was too steep and too slippy, to say nothing of it being too close to the very edge of a considerable sheer drop.

But I had the awful feeling that the horse I chose to ask might look at me with horror or disdain, and decline.

What would I do then? Ask another, less discerning equine the same question? Risk another embarrassing refusal?

I stared hard at the little group of horses. They stared back. Tod thought it was funny.

The moment of truth. Would I ask one to carry me part way up? Or would I give it a go under my own steam? I dithered, expertly.

But finally I couldn't do it. I just couldn't do it. I can honestly say that part of the reason for my decision to attempt the whole climb up to the Monastery without help, was fear of equine refusal, of equine laughter, and fear of that look that said,

"You must be joking! You need an elephant, not a horse!"

"Come on," Tod said, and reached a hand out to me, "You can do it." His misplaced faith in my ability was touching.

I took his hand, smiled at him, and prayed he was right.

We walked on through the forest and away from the horses, who probably breathed a communal sigh of relief at my departure.

Ten minutes later we emerged from the forest again into a clearing and **WOW**! There it was. So far above us that we had to crane our necks right back to look that far up.

107

Surely there cannot be anywhere a more spectacular sight, a more majestic sight, rising from the calm peacefulness of a completely silent forest, up into the perfect blue of a clear sky above.

We stared up. We had never seen a sight like it. Tiger's Nest. Remarkable. Truly a marvel. The mountain face upon which the Monastery balances is mostly bare rock, which is itself unusual, as the whole area around is almost completely covered in forest right up to the mountain peaks.

Taktsang Palphug Monastery (Tiger's Nest) was built in 1692 around the cave where Guru Padmasambhava is said to have meditated for three years, three months, three weeks, three days and three hours, in the eighth century. The Guru is credited with the introduction of Buddhism to Bhutan, and is also known as the 'Second Buddha'.

A couple of very large black birds floated around on the currents, circling each other just about on a level with the Monastery. They looked like moving black specs at that height.

I had a moment of panic. My breathing refuses to work on any upward inclination, and believe me, this wasn't just 'any' upward inclination – this was the side of your house.

And of course, taking deep breaths doesn't achieve a great deal because there isn't as much oxygen in the air at that altitude – 10,000ft.

My heart sank. I knew I wouldn't get up there. Surely only mountaineers and mad people climb up to the Temple. And Buddhist monks, who spend a month getting up there, and then never come back down. Why would they?

Tod grabbed my hand and set off at a disgustingly brisk pace, dragging me after him. We began the climb. It was a beautiful, warm morning, just perfect for a stroll through the Himalayas.

We seemed to be strangely alone on the steep, rocky track. I wondered where everyone was. I struggled grimly on with Tod by my side, urging my feet to do the one in front of the other bit, and in no time at all I was muttering darkly, gasping for air, and sweating like a champion racehorse. Our two guides, who we had found waiting for us perched on a rocky outcrop, like two garden gnomes, eventually gave up tut tutting sympathetically and trotted on ahead,

"See you at the Canteen," they said, "We will get lunch for you."

We eventually realised that we had been late starting the climb, and began to pass a steady trickle of fellow climbers who'd already reached their marvellous goal, and were now descending.

They were in various stages of sweaty exhaustion, although none as bad as I was. That really didn't bode well, and there was a great deal of sympathy and encouragement extended in my direction!

Now I've said it before, but I really do have to say it again – if you want an ice breaker in any part of the world, in any culture, in any situation, take a Tod with you. It's not just the beard; it's the smile above it too.

There was not a group, not an individual that we passed who did not stop and chat, shake hands, smile, laugh. I was glad. It gave me extra time to try to catch my breath!

The views from the steep mountain track began to touch on the spectacular, as the forest below moved further and further away. But we couldn't see Tiger's Nest – it was still too far above us.

As I have said, the Monastery is built over caves in the rock face where monks meditated in ages past. It has been rebuilt twice over the years, following destruction by fires. The last fire was blamed on villagers who, having harvested their crops in the valley below Tiger's Nest, at the base of the cliff, then set fire to the stubble. Whether or not a spark or glowing ember actually travelled on the air currents so far up the mountain as to set fire to the

Monastery will never be known, but the villagers accepted responsibility for the destruction of Taktsang Palphug Monastery, and rebuilt it in exactly the same style.

Two hours later; two sweaty hours of forcing my legs to move and my lungs to do their job, we reached the Horse Car Park. Half a dozen horses were parked there, so it would seem that half a dozen humans had been lucky enough to hitch a ride thus far.

The Canteen was just a couple of minutes further on. Our guides were waiting there for us, and there were about a dozen assorted tourists sitting round, enjoying lunch and a well-earned rest.

We sat down at a wooden table outside the spacious wooden dining house. The lads brought us cold lemonade, and grinned at my hot, red face and sweat soaked tee shirt. I grinned back.

We sat drinking the lemonade and staring across a deep ravine at the Monastery. We were on the *same* level as that wonderful building, and felt we could reach out and touch it; it appeared to be so close. It was breath taking.

The bright sunshine bounced off the cream coloured walls and golden, sloping, tiered roofs of the Temple. The brisk mountain breeze blew the dozens of strings of prayer flags that waved out over the sheer cliff, sending their prayers up to heaven with each flap of a colourful square.

A feeling of deep peace, of oneness with the Absolute seemed to permeate the air. I wanted to stay there for ever, breathing it in.

However, in order to actually *reach* the Monastery we had to cross the ravine that separated us from Tiger's Nest, and in order to do that we had to descend quite a considerable distance, and then ascend the other side,

"Don't you worry," a lovely American fellow climber told me, "The steps are next, and they're the easy bit! It's steps down, and then steps up, and then, guess what! *You're there!* You can do it!" and she grinned a huge

Cheshire cat grin, patted me on the back, and trotted off down the path.

Right oh.

We ate a wonderful lunch while I whinged about being a condemned man....and blamed Tod for everything, I usually do. He just ignores me.

From that point on we were alone on our climb – everyone else had finished and gone on down the mountain. They called friendly encouragement, and waved to us as they went,

"It's alright for *them*; they've done it!" I said peevishly, "They'll be home and in the bath before we even reach the Monastery!"

We hadn't realised we were so late, but the guides told us not to worry because we had plenty of time, and off they went like a couple of gazelles on speed, down the seemingly endless span of stone steps leading to the bottom of the ravine.

I puffed, panted and sweated, but was absolutely determined to get up to Tiger's Nest. I did not want to see an 'I told you so' expression on any horse's face.

Finally, another two hours later, we reached the Temple and stood in awe in front of the Buddha there. We gazed into the small, dark cave below the Temple's stone floor, where over the ages devoted monks have locked themselves away, and remained deep in meditation for impossible lengths of time.

We stared down from the unprotected edge of the cliff face, and winced at the sheer drop below. The wild, cold and unpredictable wind whipped across our faces, and I wondered at the dedication of the eleven Buddhist monks who live permanently in Taktsang Palphug Monastery. I envied them their peace.

As you might expect, there is little to see inside the area of the Temple which is open to the public, and the monks who live there have no comforts, save the knowledge that they are truly closer to God.

Our two young guides did not bother to wait for us, and having seen us safely into the Monastery they set off back down the mountain at a fast clip, obviously assuming that it would take me another four hours at least to reach ground level again. Probably a fair assumption, given the sweat soaked, stumbling wreck that they had delivered to Tiger's Nest.

Ha! Imagine their guilty surprise when Tod and I trotted into the forest clearing at the mountain's base no more than thirty minutes after *them*!

They were sitting in the car, and jumped in fright and switched their mobile phones off when we knocked on the window. They both stared goggle eyed at me, as if Tod had descended the mountain with another woman! We grinned.

Going down is nothing like as difficult for me as going up. It could have something to do with gravity, who knows, but I was barely out of breath and thoroughly enjoyed the descent. Can't say the same for the ascent though.

Tod and I stood for a while in silence at the edge of the forest, unwilling to take our leave.

Tiger's Nest, that Gem, that Marvel, is indelibly printed on our memories. We thanked the happy chance that had posted a certain magazine, with a certain fabulous cover photo, through our door one cold and rainy winter's day in England.

Taktsang Palphug Monastery – truly a sight to see before you die.

CHAPTER FOURTEEN

Having decided to visit Bhutan on this trip, in order to climb up to Tiger's Nest, it crossed my mind as I sat in front of my computer at home in the UK, that it would be nice to *drive* back to Nepal via India; that way we would be able to see so much more of the country than if we simply flew back.

Entry and exit from Bhutan are strictly controlled, and there is only one border crossing in the south into India, at the town of Phuentsholing. So, before we left England, I arranged for a car and driver to take us down to the Indian border on the last day of our stay in Bhutan. However, the already complicated process of getting our Visas for Bhutan then became more complicated because we needed a 'road permit' in order to leave the country by car.

More emails, more scanning of documents, more payments.

I trawled the internet looking for the best way to find a car and driver *in* India, to take us to Nepal. Could we arrange that before we got to the border? Hummm. And where was the border crossing from India into Nepal?

I stared, Gollum-like, at maps of Bhutan, India, and Nepal on the internet; checking distances, reading other travellers' experiences, looking for border crossings, wondering about our best route.

And *then* …. I noticed Darjeeling.

A light bulb went on in my brain, illuminating an enticing series of possibilities. Well, well. Darjeeling is really not far at all from the west of Bhutan, and we would be travelling in the right direction if we went there, i.e. towards Nepal. Well, more or less. Roughly the right direction. Sort of.

I just *knew* that Tod would be thrilled to spend some time in Darjeeling. *Why?* Because the *Himalayan Toy*

Train is there of course! I felt a bit of an adventure coming on. Yippee!

More Visas, more scanned documents, more payments.

We stayed the night of our Tiger's Nest climb, our last night in Bhutan, in a Meditation Centre in the mountains on the outskirts of Paro. It seemed to be built entirely of wood, and our room for the night was an isolated wooden 'mini chalet' at the back of the main building, reached by a steep, external wooden stairway.

The room was lovely, but cold. It began to rain in true Himalayan monsoon fashion as we arrived, and the stunning mountain view from the windows quickly became a view of almost ground level cloud, and wind lashed trees and prayer flags.

The wind found its cunning way through every gap in the woodwork around the room, and there were more gaps in that room than hairs on a Yeti.

Our two guides had checked us in, and shown us to our room. They told us where to find the dining room, and then said,

"Have a good evening. We will pick you up at four tomorrow to drive to the border," and they started to close the door,

"Four?" I said, "Isn't that a bit late? Wouldn't it be better to leave earlier?"

"No, no," they said, "The border crossing closes at twelve, so we will have time."

"Twelve?" Tod and I looked at each other, "But I don't think it's a good idea to arrive in India at twelve o'clock. We've got to find a taxi," I said, "and that may not be too easy at midnight."

"No, no, not midnight! Mid*day*! The border closes at midday on a Sunday," they said, "And it is Sunday tomorrow, so we will collect you here at four o'clock in the morning," and grinning, (wickedly, I thought) they closed the door and left. We heard them chatting and laughing as they clattered down the stairs outside.

I was devastated,

"I'm tired!" I whinged, "I need my sleep. I've just climbed Tiger's Nest! I'll *never* manage to get up that early!" and I plonked down on the edge of the bed and considered the merits of squeezing out a tear or two,

"Yes you will," Tod said, "Come on; let's go get something to eat," and he opened the door and stood waiting, thereby allowing the brisk, wet breeze to make itself at home in our room. I dragged myself reluctantly off the bed and trundled over to the door,

"Come on," Tod said, putting his arm round me, "You'll feel better when you've eaten."

He was right of course, as usual, and the food, served to us in the wooden dining room, was very good!

By the time we settled down for what would be a short night, that breeze had become a veritable gale, thrashing raindrops against the windows like pebbles, and howling as it tried to rip the room apart. It was accompanied by booming thunder that rolled, echoed and crashed around the mountains behind the Meditation Centre. It was quite dramatic, and kept us awake until the wee small hours.

Four in the morning found us perched in semi darkness on a wall outside the Centre, admiring the colours in the sky that heralded the coming of a calm, Himalayan dawn. It was warm, and only the occasional puddle here and there bore witness to the night's apocalyptic storm. It had passed, leaving a fresh new day in its wake.

We asked the guides how long the drive to the Indian border would take,

"We must be there before midday," they told us. So, no specifics there then, but we knew that Bhutan is a very small country, usually described as being about half the size of the American state of Indiana. It is roughly 190 miles from its eastern border to its western border, and roughly 90 miles north to south. Shouldn't take long, we thought.

So off we set to drive south through the Land of the Thunder Dragon.

It was a wonderful, memorable drive, along narrow, well-constructed roads, that somehow managed to take us up and over steep, thickly forested mountains, and down into deep green valleys.

The countryside was pristine, primeval, seemingly untouched by any kind of human development, and we passed no villages, no habitations, and no other cars. We drove on through the bright morning sunshine beneath a cloudless deep blue sky. Perfect.

We did see an occasional patch of cultivated land, and the guides told us that rice, potatoes and mushrooms were grown in Bhutan, but everything else was imported from India, or through India. We had sampled some of the mushrooms and found them to be very tasty, though hard to take too seriously, as they resembled a larger version of Yoda's ears!

"Do you have a sunroof on your car in the UK?" one of the lads asked, turning round in the passenger seat to face us,

"Err, yes," Tod said,

"That must be good, to be driving with the sunroof open?"

"It rains a bit too much in England! But yes, it's good from time to time," Tod said,

"We are not allowed to have an open sunroof at any time," the young man said, "Because of the landslides, the rocks falling…."

"Ah," we said, and I began to examine the road around for evidence of rock falls. There was plenty to be seen, and in one area we had to actually drive carefully round a pile of boulders in the road, which must have fallen from the mountain above,

"How often do rocks fall on cars?" I asked nervously, hoping for the right answer,

"It happens," he said, "Yes, it happens."

Wrong answer.

Our progress was not fast along those high, winding roads, which is just as well really, because we rounded a bend in the middle of nowhere and came nose to nose with three large, black cars. Our driver stood on the brakes and we screeched to a halt, throwing Tod and me forward against the front seats.

We gathered ourselves together, and noticed that our two guides had both dropped their heads onto their chests, and were sitting perfectly still and quiet, looking down.

The convoy of black cars, which had paused momentarily as we appeared round the bend right in front of it, now moved off again. The three cars drove past us, their heavily tinted windows glinting in the sunshine, obscuring any view of those within.

Tod and I looked at each other. Initially, when we had skidded to a stop, I thought we had hit an animal on the road, and Tod thought the convoy may have been escorting a prisoner somewhere.

But no. Guess what. The King of Bhutan was in the middle car! Cool.

As time went on we began to notice that we were driving faster, and rightly assumed that we were behind schedule. We weren't exactly doing wheelies around corners, but we did have to hang on in the back seat!

I wondered what would happen if we missed the border crossing, if it was closed when we arrived. Would they ask us for another $250US each? Hummm. Or would they smuggle us across the border at some remote spot....or maybe lock us in the car for the night?

"Stop a moment," Tod said, "Let's just have a look over there," and he pointed down into a massive, flat floored, steep sided valley.

We were high above it, and had a bird's eye view of the brick factories and other industries in the valley that were belching out thick, dark trailers of smoke. We were shocked.

It was the huge cloud of yellowish pollution, of filthy smog, hanging over the valley that had caught Tod's attention,

"What's that?" he asked the guides,

"This is the last valley before the border," they said, "And this is where we have our industry."

We got out of the car and stood at the side of the road, looking down. All around, the high, forested peaks of the Himalayas watched us without sound, and nothing moved except a group of massive birds that seemed to hang in the air, very near the top of one of the mountains. Their cries reached us faintly on a gentle breeze,

"But....Look at the pollution," we said. We were horrified, "Are there no controls on emissions? Is there no regulation?"

It was all the more shocking because it was so very unexpected. The two guides shook their heads, and looked away from the valley,

"Our government cannot do anything about it," they told us, "It is too late. It is out of control."

What? What on earth were we talking about here? What did they mean, 'too late', and 'out of control'?

And although it was hard to tell for sure, it did seem as if our young guides did not view the pollution in the valley as any great potential problem, or even as something that merited any action. After all, the site was near the country's southern border, away from the capital city and areas of population in Bhutan.

Out of sight, out of mind? Maybe.

They certainly did not want to pursue the subject, and got back in the car, ready to continue our journey.

We were stunned. I suppose we were also naïve, but the sight of that dreadfully polluted valley, coming as it did after hours of driving through clear, fresh air, and wonderfully untainted scenery, saddened and depressed us, and has remained etched painfully across our memories. Was our previously held image of Bhutan flawed?

The Indian town of Jaigaon, in West Bengal, is the gateway into India from the Bhutanese border town of Phuentsholing. It is not large, having a population of roughly 28,000, but it is certainly thriving.

We drove slowly through the small town of Phuentsholing, along the neat, clean road that led to India. We passed through a massive, wooden gateway....and entered a totally different world!

It was as if some god, with rather an odd sense of humour, was having a laugh with us, and had picked us up and dropped us into a boiling cauldron, which was already full to bursting with the whole kit and caboodle!

We found ourselves on a square which was crammed to overflowing with men, women, children, cows, goats, cars, bicycles, boxes, handcarts....All of life seemed to be represented there, and the noise it was making was deafening. It was wonderful!

The sun beat down on a veritable scrum, through which we could move only very, very slowly. We gawped out the car window in awe as the commotion rolled past.

We eventually reached the other side of the square, and stopped next to half a dozen battered looking cars, which turned out to be taxis. Their half dozen drivers were sitting together at the side of the road smoking.

Now what you don't want to do; actually, what you *really* don't want to do, is to approach half a dozen Indian taxi drivers who have no work on, and say,

"How much to Darjeeling?" in a very polite English voice.

119

Bit of a mistake really. But we live and learn, don't we? And anyway, the guides sorted it out and rescued me,

"We will take you to the passport check now," they said, "and then bring you back to your taxi." I felt like a naughty five year old who needed to be supervised!

How anyone ever finds the three separate places, which a tourist is required to attend for the passport check, is one of the world's greatest mysteries. I fear we would have been there now, still searching, passports clutched in sweaty hands, if not for the lads.

But from the moment we entered India, leaving behind us that clean and peaceful other world, that serene country of Bhutan, it was obvious that our guides were uncomfortable, to say the least. It was also obvious that they couldn't wait to leave.

So we said a very brief farewell to them, as they dropped us off beside our taxi, and waved goodbye as they somehow turned the car, and zig zagged off across the square, avoiding here a wandering cow, there a running child, back to their own beloved country, and to their share of its Gross National Happiness.

CHAPTER FIFTEEN

Before we left the UK I had searched the internet for a rough estimate of the cost of taking a taxi from Jaigaon to Darjeeling. I even checked the figure with our Bhutanese tour company. I was confident that it seemed to be around $60 or $70US, certainly no more than that.

Before we actually reached the border at Phuentsholing our guides suggested that an Indian 'friend' of theirs would be happy to take us to Darjeeling for $120US,

"That's quite expensive," I said, "It seems to be about $70US at the most for the trip,"

"Ah, but the *extra* money is for a *big* car, with plenty of room, so you can relax," they said,

"We can relax in a small car," I said, grinning,

"And the *extra* money is for a *most* comfortable car," they said, "because the road up to Darjeeling is very rough,"

"Not to worry," I said, "we're used to bumpy journeys,"

"This journey will be more than bumpy. It is a *very* bad road!" they said,

"That's ok," I said, "We'll manage," and I ignored the sideways look that Tod gave me.

So we shook hands with the Indian taxi driver, agreed to pay him the $65US he had asked for, and got into his small Suzuki.

Off we went; on what he told us would be a five or six hour drive to Darjeeling. We were thrilled. Another adventure!

It probably took us as long as five minutes to realise that we were being driven by a madman.

He was actually a very pleasant madman, and kept turning round to ask us questions about the UK, and considering the speed we were hurtling along at, that was quite some feat.

By that I mean it was 'quite some feat' that we didn't squash any men, women, children or animals during the time he wasn't watching the road ahead. Actually, it was also quite some feat that we didn't squash any men, women, children or animals during the time he **was** watching the road ahead. Because he drove fast. Very fast indeed.

I ended up staring permanently out of the side window, as I could not bear to look ahead. I **knew** we were going to hit something, somewhere along that immensely crowded road. I would have put money on it, as we were travelling in excess of 100 kmph! Tod took a photo of the speedo, although how he managed to keep his hands still for long enough to focus is a mystery, as the car swerved and skidded along the road, and **we** swerved and skidded in sympathy with it on the backseat.

Suddenly, after about half an hour of miraculous near misses, we turned sharply right onto another road,

"It will get a little bumpy now, I'm sorry," our pleasant maniac shouted to us, "But just for five kilometres."

Well, *'a little bumpy'* didn't do justice to the series of massive craters, gullies, and rocks that we then encountered. We crashed along on a road surface that rivalled the surface of the moon, with an occasional patch of flat, sandy, *slippy* surface in between. Not an inch of tarmac anywhere.

Our heads hit the car roof so often that it's a wonder we didn't knock ourselves out,

"Hummm. This must be the 'rough' road our guides mentioned," I thought, wondering how we'd have fared had we taken the '*mos*t comfortable' car instead. Not that much better, I suspected.

It was *so* bad that we began to laugh. We couldn't help it. What else could we do?

The 'road' for want of a better word, was wide and straight, and crossed a flat, dry area of land that extended as far as the eye could see on both sides. There were clumps of tall trees here and there, and crops that looked like sugar cane growing beneath the scorching sun. It seemed to be mostly an area of sporadically occurring jungle vegetation, and it was hot.

The route was obviously an important one for trade and commerce, and huge, brightly painted trucks with loud horns and laughing drivers mingled with all manner of cars and smaller trucks as if they were dodgems, avoiding each other by the skin of their teeth, swerving across the road to the wrong side, to drive along a flat patch, then skidding and screeching back to the other side again.

It was a scene of good humoured mayhem, for everywhere you looked drivers and passengers were smiling – it was obviously the Indian equivalent of fairground bumper cars, and it was *fun*!

"You must not drive along this road at night," our driver yelled above the cacophony of roaring engines and clanging, stressed metal, "It is a crossing place for jungle animals!" and as if to underline what he had said the traffic stopped suddenly, to allow an elephant to cross the road in front of us.

I wondered where it was going, that most majestic of animals; what kind of life it led, and what it thought of the humans who had built a road of sorts right through its territory, encroaching on its privacy, and on its right to live a peaceful life.

We drove over several bridges spanning vast, empty river beds, and passed massive stretches of bone dry land, where the hot breeze whipped up little tornadoes of sandy soil, played with them for a while, then dropped them.

We wondered at the empty rivers. It was the end of March. Wasn't that a bit early in the year for parched river beds?

Eventually the countryside outside the car windows began to change. It became greener, more fertile. We began to notice tea plantations alongside the road, and we started to see mountains in the misty distance ahead,

"Darjeeling!" our driver said, grinning and jabbing a finger towards them,

"How high is Darjeeling?" Tod asked me,

"Oh, it's about 1,000ft," I told him, "Not high."

Now where on earth did I get *that* gem of information from? Obviously, I had researched Darjeeling on the internet in the UK, but possibly I wasn't wearing the right reading glasses at the time.

Three or four hours into the journey we began to climb up into the mountains, and the road suddenly became full of very large, black four by fours, with sinister, tinted windows,

"Look at them!" our driver said, pointing to the cars, "They are taking tourists to Sikkim. They always drive black four by fours."

I wanted to ask who 'they' were, and I wanted to ask *why*, but I thought better of it. The road was narrow, winding, and steep, so it was probably better if our driver actually watched it as he drove.

We soon became wedged in amongst a positive convoy of the large black cars, and crawled slowly upwards along the mountain road, an ant amongst dinosaurs,

"We turn off here!" our driver suddenly yelled, and we shot off the main road onto an even narrower, *very* steep and *very* winding road. In no time at all we were stuttering along in first gear as the little car, with its little engine, did its best to get us to our destination,

"Aren't we a bit higher than 1,000ft?" Tod asked,

"We'll probably start dropping down a bit now," I told him confidently, nodding wisely.

It turned out to be the old colonial road, and no one else seemed to know it existed. We were alone on it. The road wound upwards through a forest, and although we knew we were going up and up, we did not know exactly where we were,

"Look!" the driver said, stopping the car, "It's a new hydroelectric dam," and he pointed to a gap in the trees through which we could see the dam under construction far below. Actually, *very* far below. More than 1,000ft below.

We drove on, and suddenly we were there. In Darjeeling,

"Is this only 1,000ft?" Tod asked innocently, "Seems a bit higher than that, don't you think?" and he looked at me, waiting.

I gave him one of my withering stares, reserved for those times when I think *he* may be right, and *I* may be wrong.

Actually, Darjeeling is located in the Himalayan foothills, in the Indian State of West Bengal, at an altitude of 6,710ft (2,045m). Yes, I *did* apologise to Tod. He just smiled.

Darjeeling became a resort, a 'hill station', in the mid nineteenth century, and developed as a Victorian town following the establishment of a sanatorium and a military base there by the colonial British. It was, for them, a popular holiday destination due to its pleasant climate, and wonderful views of the gently rolling Himalayan foothills. Darjeeling became known as 'the summer capital of India' in the days of the Raj.

The Darjeeling Himalayan Railway (The Toy Train) was opened in 1881 and is now a Unesco World Heritage Site. It is a 2ft narrow gauge railway (that's a dinky train to you and me) that runs from Darjeeling to New Jalpaiguri, along 78km of track. There are regular daily trips by the small, really cute, steam locomotives to Ghum, India's highest railway station.

And *that* was why we went to Darjeeling! Yea!

CHAPTER SIXTEEN

We loved Darjeeling!

Our hotel was pretty central, and we drove along the town's narrow bustling streets, past shops crowded with colourful goods and equally colourful shoppers; past market stalls piled high with pashminas, Indian and western clothes, and all kinds of interesting foods; and of course past the multitude of shops selling tea. You'd expect that in Darjeeling, a town known for, and surrounded by tea plantations!

There is quite a large Tibetan population in the town, and our hotel was owned and run by a Tibetan couple who had escaped from the Tibet Autonomous Region many years before, and journeyed to Darjeeling.

Our driver neatly avoided a family of monkeys with no knowledge of the Highway Code, who crossed the road in front of us, and deposited us at the hotel door. We thanked him very much. He was still smiling as he drove away.

Our stay began well. The hotel couldn't find our booking, so the manager himself drove us to another, much posher hotel, which they also owned, and we stayed the night there!

The next day we set off on foot to explore Darjeeling. The sun was shining, it was pleasantly warm, the air was fresh and clear, and within a very short time we felt we could have been in the Lake District of England, a hundred and fifty years ago. We walked along pleasant, hilly roads lined with leafy trees; we walked past rambling, English-style houses from past centuries, with neat gardens and flower beds in front, encircled by metal railings stamped with 'made in London'. Wow!

Most signs and house names were in English, including the wonderful 'Windermere Hotel'. That really tickled us!

Darjeeling is attractive. It sprawls across a series of Himalayan foothills, and is surrounded by hillside after hillside covered in tea plantations. Possibly the most endearing thing about the town itself is that you undoubtedly walk in the footsteps of those who have gone before, and who have left behind such a massive legacy.

We walked past a wooden pavilion, which must surely once have been a cricket pavilion, but was now the 'Darjeeling Library'. We stepped up onto the veranda and went in to ask the smiling librarian if we could look round.

We tip toed around on the old wooden floor, staring at the old books stacked on the old wooden shelves and lying on the old wooden tables, wondering at the collection, wondering if these amazing books had been left there by the British. The pavilion contained mainly English language books, atlases and dictionaries, many of them over one hundred years old. We spent a long and pleasant time nosing round.

Up on a steep hill, overlooking the pleasant leafy area we were walking round, was a Church. It could only have been brought, brick by brick, from England!

We climbed the hill and stopped in front of the sign that said 'St Andrew's Church'. The times of the services were listed below. Oh wow.

We walked on, up to the wrought iron gates leading into the neat, grassy area that surrounded the church. There was no one in sight, but the gates were unlocked, so we pushed them open and went in. It was very peaceful up there; the only sound was birdsong.

We walked slowly round the front of the church, admiring it, oddly aware that we could have been walking round a church in the UK. That thought was somehow almost disorienting.

We tried the huge wooden doors with the circular, shiny metal door handles, but they were locked. We were disappointed. We had hoped to see inside.

We continued slowly on round the church to the back, hoping maybe there was another, unlocked door to be found.

We came across a small house there, at the back of the church, and ducked under the line of washing hanging outside it. We knocked on the door, hoping to find a caretaker to let us in to see the church. But there was no answer, so we walked slowly back to the front again, and stood looking down the hill and out across the town of Darjeeling. The view was wonderful from that vantage point.

A couple of minutes later a man appeared from the direction of the small house. He didn't seem surprised to see us there, and smiled at us. By the use of hand signs and laughter we got him to understand that we'd like, if possible, to see inside the church. We were in luck. He *was* the caretaker, and he rooted through his jacket pocket, eventually producing a massive, ornate key which could not have been anything other than the key to the church. We followed him round the building, where he opened a side door for us, and we stepped inside. The caretaker smiled and left us to browse.

There was a wonderfully peaceful atmosphere inside the church, and a smell of dust mingled with old wood. We became instantly aware that we had stepped back through the centuries. The old wooden floorboards and severe wooden pews had probably not changed since the church had first opened its doors to the worshipping colonial British.

The sunlight slanted through the high windows, catching the dancing, airborne dust in its rays, and dappling the walls with patches of vibrant reds and greens stolen from the old stained glass.

We walked slowly round, looking at the abundance of plaques hanging on the walls. They told heart wrenching stories of lives lived as tea plantation managers, of young and gallant soldiers, and of so many lives cut tragically short by hitherto unknown disease, or by armed conflict.

The names were shockingly familiar. They were English, Scottish, and Welsh names, written carefully, with love and anguish, on a church wall in a distant, far flung corner.

The organ was at the back of the church, and it was amazing. I spotted a notice pinned to the wall above it, the faded ink writing on yellowing paper explaining that it had first been played on 1st April 1877,

"Guess what," I said to Tod, "It's the 1st April today!" We sang happy birthday to the organ. I'm sure it appreciated that.

The caretaker came in, wondering if we were still there and, realising how interested we were in the church and its history, he began to point out items of special interest that he thought we may have missed, such as the original, round metal light switches with 'made in England' stamped on them. We all giggled, and we discovered that his English was pretty good; much better than our Bengali!

We spent well over an hour wandering round, taking photos and chatting with him, and then we said goodbye.

We walked slowly back down the steep path to the road at the bottom of the hill, turned and looked back up at the church, in much the same way as I suppose the colonial British would have done on a Sunday, so very long ago,

"Can you see the clothes line?" Tod asked me,

"Err, yes," I said, squinting through the sunshine,

"Just watch," he said, and so I did.

There were half a dozen white cloths hanging from the line. They were rather like tea towels, the same shape and size, and there was a heavy, multi coloured rug on the end. Nothing was kept in place by clothes pegs, and the cloths and rug were simply doubled over the clothes line.

As we watched, a monkey climbed a nearby wall and leapt onto the line. It tottered about for a moment, trying to get its balance, hanging on with all four feet. I realised that there was already a monkey on the line. That was the one Tod had spotted. The pair obviously had a cunning plan. They took hold of the first cloth, yanked it hard until it came off the line, and then threw it down onto the grass below. They moved on to the next one, and the next! Pretty soon the line was almost bare. Only the rug remained. But the pair couldn't budge it; it was too heavy for them. They didn't give up though, and disappeared underneath it. The rug moved and bobbed up and down on the line, while the intrepid pair pushed, pulled and shoved. Eventually the rug slipped too far down one side, and gravity stepped in to help the vandals. It fell heavily to the ground.

The caretaker came out of his house, saw what had happened to his washing, and simply picked everything up and put it back on the line. No annoyance; no frown. The culprits sat in a nearby tree and watched. I suspected they were grinning.

We walked on around the sometimes steep narrow streets, absolutely fascinated to see the remnants of British colonial occupation everywhere we looked. We walked through the newly renovated Nightingale Park; we went into the old chemist shop with the original wooden floorboards and massive, round clock on the wall behind the old wooden counter; and we walked past 'Little Big Ben'.

Of course we gravitated towards the Darjeeling Himalayan Railway Toy Train Station, and stood watching in awe, as the tiny steam locomotives puffed backwards and forwards. The train lines run through the town, along and across the streets, within touching distance of the shops, and squashing distance of the unwary.

We took photos, and the drivers asked Tod to hop on board and have a look. He did!

Unfortunately, all the five steam trains were just being laid up for repairs, so for the next week only diesel trains were running. Pity. But we would still enjoy the ride. We planned to buy our tickets the next day.

We wandered round the backstreets of Darjeeling, and everywhere we went people said hello, and asked if they could take photos of us. I think Tod's beard had a lot to do with it!

We found a small road which had been named after the British botanist J. D. Hooker, who spent time in the Himalayas, and in Darjeeling, in the 1840s. We followed it downwards and passed the house where he had set up his laboratory, the house that looked as if it should have been on a hillside in the Lake District.

There were plenty of street dogs in Darjeeling. The Indian street dogs have a greyhound-style body, with longish faces and short fur. We noticed that several of them were plump. Odd that, plump street dogs.

Continuing on along Hooker Street, we found ourselves walking down a very steep pathway, past a row of cottages straight out of Wales. The warm sun shone on the pink climbing roses that grew over the cottage doors and small wooden fences in front of them.

A group of half a dozen Indian ladies, wearing colourful saris, were sitting on the ground outside the cottages, and around them were probably about seven or eight dogs lying quietly, sunbathing.

Tod and I said hello, and I asked if the dogs were theirs,

"No," one of the ladies told us, "They are street dogs. They don't belong to anyone, but we look after them and feed them."

It was a lovely moment, and I found myself wishing that the Nepalese people felt the same about *their* dogs.

Further down the path we passed a dog alone. I found a biscuit left over from lunch, and held it out to him. He took it from me gently and began to munch. I said,

"Good boy," and he suddenly stopped munching and stared hard at me, with an unmistakable expression of suspicion on his face. I was taken aback. Then he actually *spat out* what was left of the biscuit, and walked off without a backward glance. That's *me* off his Christmas card list.

Interesting though, isn't it? Why did he do that? Was he not familiar with the English words, and did he maybe think I was trying to poison him?

The next day we decided to go sightseeing further afield, and paid the hotel for a standard day trip with a car and driver. When the car arrived, guess what? Not only was our driver a Liverpool Football Club supporter, but he was undoubtedly the only headbanger (lover of loud rock music!) in Darjeeling! We set off down the road with red Liverpool FC scarves flying from the car windows, and heavy metal music thumping in our ears. We were unable to do anything but laugh.

He took us first to a Tea Garden – a Tea Plantation to you and me. Sadly, I have to say that it was probably the least attractive place we saw in the Darjeeling area. It was full of tourists, which in itself was no big deal; after all, what were *we*? But it was noisy, dirty and *ultra-commercial*. There were several stalls there renting out, for the purpose of the tourists' photos, what the stall holders assured everyone was 'authentic Indian clothing, as worn by the tea pickers in the time of the Raj'.

We were really disappointed. We had hoped to be able to look round the plantation house, which we could see in the distance behind a group of tea trees, but it was closed.

However, we spent the rest of the day very pleasantly, driving round the area, stopping here and there, getting a feel for the place,

"I'll pick you up at four in the morning!" our young driver said, as we got out of the car later that day at the end of our tour,

"What on earth for?" we asked him, wondering if he was joking,

"To go to Tiger Hill Observatory. You'll be able to see the sun rise over the mountains. It's beautiful," he said, but with no real conviction in his voice. I suspected he had seen the sun rise over the mountains so many times that its attraction had waned somewhat; or maybe our young man didn't really want to get up so early. *I was with him there*; I hadn't forgotten Bhutan and our 4am ordeal!

Tod looked as if he may have been going to say,

"Ok, 4am is good," but I nipped that madness in the bud,

"No way! Perish the thought!" I said, "We'd like to go there, but not at 4am!"

"See you at eight then!" the young man shouted happily, and drove off in a loud flurry of Led Zeppelin, and dangling, flapping football scarves. Yes, I reckon he was more than pleased to have a couple of extra hours in bed!

But we were *so* glad we *hadn't* struggled out of bed in the early hours of the morning. Because it was pretty awful at Tiger Hill Observatory.

Tiger Hill is 11km from Darjeeling, and is famous for its views of Mount Everest and Kanchenjunga, which is India's highest mountain, and the world's third highest mountain. It is known as 'the five treasures of snow' because it has five high peaks.

Tiger Hill, at 8,500ft high, is a Unesco Heritage site.

The Observatory is a four storey, glass walled, circular building, right at the top of the hill, and when we arrived there, after the statutory bumpy journey along the steep track up the sparsely forested hill, it was closed. It actually looked as if it had been closed for a very long time, and was beginning to fall into disrepair. One or two of the windows were cracked, and the wind had begun to make inroads at the edges of the frames, loosening them, threatening to rip them out.

We were the only visitors, and there was an almost mournful atmosphere as we walked round the site, as if it was yearning for the good times long since lost. The stiff breeze was cold, and blew a broken door noisily backwards and forwards at the base of the observatory building. Somehow that desolate sound did not seem inappropriate there, in that desolate place.

The usually spectacular view from the Hill was misty and clouded, and try as we might, we could not make out either Everest or Kanchenjunga.

We spent some time talking to the lovely couple who sat, wrapped against the cold in heavy coats and blankets, at a table full of photos of the wonderful mountain scenes that we should have been able to see; scenes that we would doubtless have been able to see, had we visited Tiger Hill later in the year.

We drove back to Darjeeling in silence.

The street dogs are not the only non-human inhabitants of the town of Darjeeling. There is quite a sizeable, seemingly thriving population of monkeys there too. They tend to sit along the sides of the roads and graciously accept oranges and other goodies from those who pass. We gave some cake to a small group of monkeys who were sitting on a low wall in the sunshine, next to the road. They took it enthusiastically, and ran off squabbling over portions. But when we offered the rest of the cake to a nearby street dog he just sniffed at it, stuck his nose in the air, and stalked off.

A couple of men, sitting on a bench nearby, saw what had happened and laughed,

"Don't worry, don't worry!" they said, "He is not rude, he is just not hungry! He has plenty to eat!" and we all laughed.

There was certainly a more than interesting comparison to be made between the life led by the street dogs of this part of India, and the appalling plight of the street dogs of Nepal.

But the dogs barked in the night. A veritable wall of sustained barking would roll down the mountain slopes and across the town in the darkness, night after night.

Our room was high up at the back of the hotel, overlooking a wide area of poor, one storey housing. Their flat roofs were roughly made from sections of corrugated tin, assorted pieces of wood, and plastic sheets.

A number of dogs spent the days wandering around across the roofs, or lying together in the sun there. At night they joined into groups and set off to scavenge across the town.

Finding that we had a couple of hard boiled eggs, still in their shells, left over from dinner one night, we decided to see if the dogs would like them. The sun was going down. The shadows were lengthening across the roofs, and it was getting dark, but there was still just enough light left to see the dogs beginning to gather, ready to start their night-time foraging.

We quietly opened the window as wide as we could, stood back from it to allow for strenuous overarm action, and launched the hard boiled eggs as high out over the roofs far below as we could. Yea!

We hadn't bargained for the loud noise the eggs made on landing! The booming crash of eggfall on corrugated tin echoed across the area, and we ducked down below the window like a couple of naughty kids. But the noise alerted the dogs, who raced over and duly ate the miraculous missiles.

Over the next few nights Tod perfected his egg bowling action, adding a couple of steps as a run up, and managing to launch the missiles so far out of the window that they reached the far side of the roofs. Sachin Tendulkar eat your heart out!

We went to the Toy Train Station to book tickets for a trip the next day. The queue of assorted potential travellers in front of the ticket office was massive. We stood patiently for thirty minutes in hot sunshine, and barely moved. Then an English couple in the queue ahead of us told us that we needed to fill in a form before we could even request tickets, let alone purchase them. But the form was only available from the ticket office itself. Right oh.

So, I squeezed in at the front of the queue, apologising to everyone I could see, and asked for a form. Bingo! Someone handed me one.

By the time we reached the ticket office window we were hot and frazzled, but we had the completed form in our clammy hands. The process of issuing the train tickets was **much** more complicated than landing a man on the moon, and seemed to involve writing by hand, typing on a computer, copying from the subsequent print out, arguing with other ticket clerks, and telling the waiting public that the ticket issuing system had broken down.

We waited and waited, and the man behind me in the queue began pushing me in the back. I ignored him. He pushed me some more, I ignored him some more, and he finally said, in a loud voice, bursting with exasperation,

"Madam, have you *finished*?"

I turned and glared at him,

"Why on earth would I be standing here *if I had finished*?" I asked,

"Ok," he said, and smiled. I smiled back.

It took us nearly ninety minutes to buy our tickets, but we finally had them. Yippee!

We wandered round the shopping streets in the centre of town, rubbing shoulders with other tourists, and with street sellers clutching bags and boxes piled high with pashminas, with Buddhas, and with CDs. The hordes of shoppers moved in colourful waves up and down the roads, and they all seemed to be smiling.

We spotted an 'olde worldy' English tea shop with cakes, cream buns and éclairs stacked enticingly in the window. And guess what? There was an authentic English phone box standing red, shiny and proud in the middle of the shop floor inside!

Tod walked over and started to take photos of it while I waited outside. A young Indian man came out of the shop clutching a cake which he had just bought there. I couldn't help noticing that the cake looked really lovely, with a blob of jam in the centre, and fresh cream all round the edges. Ummm. Gorgeous. Definitely an *'eat me quick'* cake.

The young man turned, held the cake out towards me, and said,

"Hummm. Well; how do you suppose I'll manage to just eat the jam, and avoid the cream?" And he smiled a very engaging smile,

"You need the services of a street dog," I told him, grinning, "There are plenty around, and if you ask politely I'm sure one of them will oblige," and we both laughed.

Tod came out of the shop putting the camera back in its case, and the young man's companions joined us. We stood in a group chatting, laughing about the phone box that looked so out of place, so....eccentric, there in the shop,

"Your English is fantastic," I said to the young man,

"It should be," he said, "I grew up in Winchester, England, and work as a barrister in London now!" We all roared with laughter.

The day of our Toy Train trip arrived. We were really excited, and got to the station in plenty of time, just in case we had to queue! We watched the trains pulling in and out, and Tod took more photos. We were not alone in having journeyed to Darjeeling just to see and ride on the Darjeeling Himalayan Railway (DHR). We met several fellow enthusiasts. The trains had been made originally in the UK, and I wondered how they had been transported all the way up to this part of India. Nowadays the Indian mechanics do a wonderful job of repairing and keeping the trains running.

But our train that day was a diesel, and we set off on time. We were going on a return trip to Ghum, India's highest railway station. The passengers were a mixture of nationalities; mostly tourists. Every seat was taken.

The tiny train chugged through the streets of Darjeeling, crossing the road here and there, passing so close to open fronted shops that you could have reached out and pinched the goods on display. People smiled and waved at the train as it passed, and we smiled and waved back.

Then we began to climb uphill through more open areas. Some of the views were spectacular out over the rolling Himalayan foothills, thickly covered in tea plantations, and sharply down into the valley far below Darjeeling. At one point the train was so close to the edge of a sheer drop that the passengers laughed nervously, and leant back from the windows!

Our train stopped for a while at the Batasia Loop. 'Batasia' means 'airy space' and the 'Loop' is literally a double loop of the Toy Train track. It was created in order for the train to be able to descend 1,000ft sharply, instead of spending ages on a gradual descent. We got out there and wandered about, admiring the flowerbeds and grassy areas that have been created inside the Loop. The War Memorial to Gorkha soldiers stands there, also inside the Loop.

Ghum Station, at an altitude of 7,407ft (2,258m) looks very much like a dilapidated English country train station from 150 years ago. Nesbit's 'The Railway Children' might have been filmed there! The train stopped at Ghum long enough for us to potter around the DHT Museum which is right there.

The trip was short, only 3.7miles (6km) and when we got back to Darjeeling we went exploring again. Wandering down a quiet side road we came across the Bengal Natural History Museum (Darjeeling). Oh boy! What a place! I'm sure it hasn't been touched in any way since the British established it in 1903!

It was an attractive, olde worldy building, probably originally a private house. We went in.

The Museum was actually one of the most fascinating places we had ever seen, but really only because the exhibits were almost certainly the originals! The place was packed to the rafters with examples of every kind of creature that had lived around the Himalayas in the early 1900s.

There was a massive crocodile in the first room we went in to, and I would swear it had been painted a dull, yellowish colour; *yes, painted*, in an attempt to cover up the fact that it was moth eaten and threadbare in a number of places, and its stuffing was hanging out.

There was stand after stand of insects. Hundreds, probably thousands of the poor creatures, which had originally been pinned carefully to the cards, but now many of them were falling apart, losing wings and legs, their bodies sagging and disintegrating through age.

Most of the information about the exhibits was clearly original, and the ink had faded badly on the old, yellowed and torn paper. And why wouldn't it? It was probably over 100 years old.

There were snakes everywhere. Big ones and small ones; poisonous ones and stuffed ones. Stuffing had obviously been all the rage at one time, and the Taxidermist's Room was packed with oddly shaped creatures, seeming slightly out of kilter now with their living relatives.

I am surprised that there are any birds left in the Darjeeling area, as so many of their ancestors were in the Museum, perched at odd angles on grimy branches everywhere you looked, feathers dull, and laden with the relentless dust of ages, their eyes bereft of the brightness of life.

But I thought the saddest room was the one containing shelf after shelf of massive glass jars containing pickled puppies, and lion and tiger cubs. I moved a small glass jar gently, trying to see what it contained, and a miniature crocodile, seemingly perfect in every way, floated slowly towards me, mouth open, tiny razor teeth visible within.

We were alone there throughout our tour round the exhibits, and we wandered about open mouthed, gawping, morbidly fascinated.

What a place.

It was a toss-up between taking a bus from Darjeeling back to Kathmandu, which would take two days and necessitate changing bus and staying overnight in the Nepali border crossing town of Kakkarvitta, or finding a car and drivers prepared to take us all the way back. Hummm.

We enquired in several tourist offices in Darjeeling, and finally found what we thought was a reasonable, safe offer - a driver who would take us all the way back to Kathmandu for roughly £200. That looked good to us, especially as he would have another driver with him, so we wouldn't need to stop at all,

"We will leave here at 6am," the driver told us with a happy smile, "and get to Kathmandu at about 7.30pm." Well, he seemed confident. What could go wrong?

We made sure we had plenty of water, fruit and a biscuit or two. We were ready to go, and really looking forward to the trip.

Yippee! Another adventure!

CHAPTER SEVENTEEN

Darjeeling was just waking up as we set off. The travel agent had promised us a comfortable car, and it was. Our driver was very pleasant, and luckily for us his English was good.

We were genuinely sorry to leave Darjeeling, and drove off through the early morning mist that crept across the hills and touched the narrow streets of the town, wondering if we would return someday.

Ten minutes later we stopped to collect our second driver. He jumped in, and nodded and smiled pleasantly at us,

"He will not be able to communicate with you because he has no English," our first driver told us, "but he can smile at you!"

Right oh. Smiling's good. But I noticed immediately that the young man had a severe turn in one eye, and wondered anxiously if that would affect his ability to drive. Did he actually have a driving license? Would he be looking at the right part of the road at the right time, so to speak? Oh dear.

We drove on in a south westerly direction, towards the Indian Nepal border crossing at Kakkarvitta, about 120km from Darjeeling. There is a customs post there, and so that is where foreigners can cross the border into Nepal.

The countryside moved gradually from cool, green mountains to much flatter, hotter land. We were headed towards the Terai, that swathe of sub-tropical plains that crosses the whole of southern Nepal, extending into India.

It grew hot in the car, and the air that blew in through the open windows was no longer refreshing. But it was a pleasant drive, with a driver who drove at a pretty reasonable speed. We felt safe.

Before we knew it,

141

"Here is the border," he said, and stopped the car. We had entered a town; quite a pleasant, bustling town, and we assumed this to be Kakkarvitta. It had taken us nearly five hours to get there,

"We will take you to the Indian customs post and come back for you later," the driver said,

"Come back for us?" we said, surprised, "How long will it take?"

"Not long," he said, and I swear his nose grew at an alarming rate, until it was brushing the windscreen.

Right oh. Customs are customs. It had to be done. There was no escape!

We pulled off the main road through large, grey stone gate posts, onto a long, winding driveway. There were gardens on both sides and we drove past tall, exotic trees and patches of long, waving grass. We left a trail of white dust hanging in the air behind us, kicked up by the tyres from the dry, gravel driveway.

A low wooden building, looking rather like a tennis pavilion, came into view. The drive became a wide, flat area in front of it, and we stopped there,

"See you later," our driver said, and his colleague smiled at us. That smile was disturbing, as the turn in his eye was indeed severe. Oh dear.

We got out,

"Do you think they'll come back for us?" I asked Tod rather nervously, as the car drove off and I looked around,

"Course they will," he grinned, "We haven't paid them yet!"

We turned towards the building which we assumed to be the customs post. There were two dogs lying on the ground outside, asleep in the sun. It was very quiet, and very, very hot,

"We'll let them lie, shall we?" I whispered, as we walked carefully round the motionless furry forms,

142

"They're the security guards," Tod whispered back, and we both giggled.

Suddenly, unexpectedly, a man in uniform stood up from where he had been sitting on the wooden veranda outside the building. He was holding a rifle in one hand, and a cigarette in the other,

"Inside," he said, and gestured behind him to an open door. He had obviously not drunk from the welcoming cup that day, but we smiled, climbed the steps up to the veranda and went in through the door he indicated. The guard followed us.

The room was small and basic. There were three or four wooden chairs in it, and a wooden table with an old fashioned phone on it,

"Sit," the uniformed man told us. We did. He remained standing.

We waited. He lit another cigarette and blew the smoke all over us. It was very quiet. We waited.

Eventually another man appeared. This one had a couple of stripes on the sleeve of his uniform. Maybe that was why he looked very severe. Maybe stripes make you severe.

Everything was done by hand, pen on paper. There was no computer, and the process took ages. We waited patiently, wondering if he knew how to smile.

Where had we been? Where were we going? How had we travelled? How were we travelling now? Where had we crossed borders?

All our answers were written down laboriously in longhand. It was very hot in the room, and the dark, unsightly patches of underarm sweat on the man's shirt grew bigger, crept closer together.

But when finally all the questioning was finished his manner changed abruptly. He smiled, chatted, asked how we liked India, how we had enjoyed Bhutan, and what we thought of Nepal. We sat nattering with him until our car drove up outside.

Then off we went again, round a corner and across a bridge. A long bridge. A very long bridge.

All manner of people, vehicles and animals were crossing the bridge which marks the border between Nepal and India. There was a slow moving line of traffic – cars, massive trucks, open backed lorries – alongside many people who were walking across the border in the, by now, searing heat. Trekkers with sweaty faces and bulging backpacks mingled with men pushing handcarts laden with goods; women leading goats pushed past women carrying wooden crates full of chickens; and families holding hands with screaming children tried to stay together in the crush.

And above all was the noise, the cacophony created by everything on that bridge, animate and inanimate. It rose into the hot, dusty air all around, as the business of the bridge, of the border, went on hour after hour.

We were glad we had decided to travel in a car rather than take a local bus. If we had taken a bus we would probably have been walking across that bridge ourselves, and I would certainly have been whingeing! It was about a kilometre long.

We needed to repeat the customs process on the Nepal side of the border. Finally reaching the end of the bridge, we drove through a wide archway, and our driver pulled in and parked almost immediately outside a building which was set some way back from the road.

We got out. The dry clay road was busy, full of people, chickens, handcarts, bicycles and young children begging. It was a chaotic scene, the kind of scene that we had become used to, if ever one *can* become used to it, in both India and Nepal.

A beautiful young girl with long dark hair and no shoes came over to us and grabbed Tod's hand,

"She says please give her some money," our driver translated, and immediately shouted at the girl, raising his hand to her, obviously threatening her. She ran off and vanished in the crowd,

"Street kid," he said and shrugged. Tod and I looked at each other. We knew better than to say anything, or to interfere. There is something of a 'zero tolerance' attitude by the population towards street children who beg from tourists, in parts of both Nepal and India.

We went into the customs building. The office was small, and a wave of trapped heat, desperate to escape, hit us as we opened the door. A man was sitting at a table behind a high wooden counter. There was a young boy standing by the counter and he grinned at us, took our proffered passports, and ran with them to the man at the table. The man at the table examined them and asked where our Visas were. The boy ran back to us with the passports and we pointed out the pages with our Visas on them. Still grinning, the boy took them back again to the man,

"We are very pleased to see you back in Nepal again," he said, smiling at us,

"Thank you," we said, "We're really happy to be back!"

I had to giggle, because when we arrived at Kathmandu airport from the UK this trip, we waited in line of course to go through Immigration, and the official we eventually saw actually remembered Tod from our two previous visits! He asked if we were going back up to the village again! How cool is that!

So we said goodbye, gave the boy some coins, and walked back to the car.

Tod said,

"Back in a moment," and vanished. I saw him across the road a few moments later, talking to the little street girl. She looked about ten years old. He gave her some money and pointed to a man sitting at the side of the road selling fruit, obviously hoping that the child would use at least some of the money to feed herself.

It's a hard one, isn't it? What to do for the best.

I got in the car, and realised with a bit of a shudder that the second driver had now got behind the wheel for the first time. Oh no. Would he be able to see both sides of the road at the same time?

However, as we had been driving slowly across the border bridge, we had both noticed that the *first* driver had developed a nervous twitch. Every so often his head would jerk violently from side to side. Maybe this involuntary action was caused by the stress of crossing the bridge so slowly in a queue, and in such intense heat. Or maybe he was prone to twitching when he was tired.

Obviously, we didn't know the reason, but coming as it did, a twitch out of the blue, it made *us* jump each time we saw it, and my nerves began to fray. What if someone crossed the road in front of the car during a twitch? What if he accidentally turned the steering wheel during a twitch, and ran into another car? Would driver number *two* be any help, or would *he* be looking somewhere else?

We set off. I feel I should report that Tod grinned at this point, and told me not to worry. Hummm.

The border town of Kakkarvitta is roughly 600kms from Kathmandu. In the scheme of things that distance means very little, as every journey is different. We were expecting, *hoping*, to get to Kathmandu by 7.30pm, and at that point in our trip it seemed likely that we would.

The land we were driving through was flat, green and open. We were crossing the Terai, the same swathe of sub-tropical, fertile lowland where Chitwan is located, and where Karma now lives at the brick factory. In fact we were not far away from her at that moment.

But we turned, and began to drive in a roughly northerly direction, towards the mountains, up towards the Himalayas, and towards Kathmandu,

"Do not worry," our driver said, "We know the way!"

Right oh. Wonder why he said that. We suspected they might *not* in fact know the way….

All around us we could see fields of sugar cane and wheat, interspersed by rice fields. We knew that tobacco, maize and jute were also grown there, but we didn't spot any.

The Terai feeds Nepal, and its importance to the country as a whole cannot be understated.

We passed water buffalo working patiently in the fields, and saw a plethora of goats wandering around, sometimes forcing the car to stop as a goatherd ushered an unruly group of them across the road.

We drove through small villages and the occasional small town, and passed many massive trucks, but relatively few cars.

We stared, fascinated and humbled, out of the windows at lives so very different from our own.

We were driving through a small town, along a wide, straight road with a surface of dusty, white, packed clay. Water buffalo were tethered all along the centre of the road. I wondered where their owners were, what they were doing while their animals were parked in the middle of the road. How odd.

The town itself was pretty quiet, with very few people walking around. So it came as something of a shock when we suddenly screeched to a halt and the driver got out and ran into a small store. We sat in curious silence and waited. When he came back a few moments later, he got in quickly, and turned the car round. The tyres kicked up a cloud of grimy, white dust as we set off back the way we had come,

"Umm, where are we going?" Tod asked,

"Short cut," the driver answered.

Right oh.

But the 'short cut' turned out to be 70km in the wrong direction! We actually drove 140km to get back to where we had started. Nothing was said about it, so *we* said nothing about it. These things happen.

We drove on and on.

Eventually we began to notice that the narrow road was climbing, and winding through forested hills. The forest began to creep nearer, to close in on the road as if the trees on either side of it were trying to touch branches across it, to hide it, and to rid themselves of this incursion into their hitherto private wilderness.

We also noticed that our drivers were stopping every so often to ask for directions! But hey ho! Not much we could do about that!

Dusk started to fall, and long, dark, oddly shaped shadows stole across the road as the mountains gradually blocked the sunshine. From that moment we began to see fires in the forests on the mountain sides above us. Just one or two small fires at first, but as we climbed higher we saw more and more.

We rounded a bend and there in the middle of the road a huge truck lay on its side. Its cargo was spread hap hazardly across the road, and smashed and splintered wooden crates, and bent and crushed cardboard boxes were strewn in all directions. The driver was sitting dejectedly amongst the debris, his head in his hands. He didn't look up as we drove slowly past. At least he didn't seem injured.

Shortly after, we passed yet another accident. This time the massive truck had skidded and hit a tree at the side of the road. The vehicle was upright, but several large branches had smashed through the windscreen, and the driver was injured and trapped in the cab. Half a dozen people were standing on the cab's battered roof, trying to cut him free, using knives and hammers. There would be no other help; no ambulance, no medics.

In all, we passed three major accidents, and a great many less serious ones,

"Raxi," our driver said. He may or may not have been right in his assumption that alcohol had caused the carnage. But it cannot be denied that Nepal has an appalling road safety record.

Every so often we crossed a bridge spanning a river. Many of the rivers were vast, and all of them were empty. There is something almost *sinister*, and certainly strangely depressing, about the sight of a completely empty river bed. Where had the water gone? Would Mother Nature replace it?

Darkness fell. We were running really late, and we started to worry about our drivers being tired. The road was now winding through high mountains covered in thick forest, and our progress had slowed considerably. We were alone on the road. Only the car's headlights illuminated our route, and we drove on through the blackness, knowing that we were passing within feet of any number of sheer drops down the mountain side along the way.

We began to see more and more forest fires on both sides of the road, some of them blazing so brightly that we could see the reflected flames dancing on our faces. In the otherwise pitch blackness the fires looked like volcanic lava pouring down the mountain side, and we could smell the smoke from them, as it blew unseen across the road in the darkness.

We rounded a tight bend and saw a village high up on the steep mountain side illuminated by savagely blazing fires above it. The houses at the top of the village had started to burn, and we could see glowing debris falling onto lower houses. They too would surely burn. We wondered where the people would go, and what would happen to their animals.

The further we went the more fires we saw, and the nearer they crept to the road. At one point we drove between blazing mountainsides, as clouds of burning embers blew across the road in front of us. Our driver put his foot down, and we shot forward,

"Don't worry!" he shouted, "We will get past the fire!"

The trees at the side of the road had caught fire. They looked like massive roman candle fireworks, as their tinder dry foliage blazed, sparked and exploded. One of them began to fall as we approached, and I grabbed Tod's hand,

"Oh my God!" I squealed. We had never seen anything like it.

We sped under the blazing, doomed tree, through a cloud of falling, burning pine cones, twigs and resin, and out the other side. The tree hit the road behind us in an explosion of bouncing sparks, far too close for comfort. I was horrified.

The forests of Nepal were ablaze. And no help was on its way. There would be no planes dropping water; no fire service clearing the area and blocking the roads. Nothing.

We had been travelling for hours and it was obvious that the drivers were tired. There had been a worrying spate of twitching from the front seat, probably anxiety based, so Tod said,

"Stop here and have a sleep. We don't mind. We'll wait."

But the drivers wanted to press on, and told us that there was not much further to go; that we were nearing Kathmandu valley. We too were tired and anxious to get to our destination, so we gave them the benefit of the doubt, after all, we really didn't have a clue where we were.

But we began to pass more and more traffic on the road, cars as well as trucks. The villages became more frequent, and we went through several police checkpoints, a sure sign that we were nearing home.

Suddenly, we were flagged down and stopped at quite a large roadblock, manned by several men in hi-vis jackets. They were not police, and we didn't understand the conversation that went on for quite some time through the car window with the drivers. We sat quietly and waited. Eventually the driver turned to us and said,

"We cannot go through because you are tourists. We have to take another route,"

"What?" I said, "What do you mean?"

"I don't know why, but they say we are not permitted to go that way because you are tourists," he said, and shrugged.

I was tired, I was hungry, and I was in no mood for this,

"I'll talk to them," I said, and I started to get out of the car,

"*You will not!*" Tod said, grabbing my arm and pinning me to the seat,

"So what's the difference in the routes?" he asked the drivers, still hanging on to my arm,

"If they let us through here we will be in Kathmandu in two and a half hours. But the way they say we have to go now, it will take at least six hours,"

"And that's because we are tourists?" Tod said,

"Yes,"

"You must be *joking*! This is *ridiculous*! Who *are* they? What do they hope to achieve?" I said, absolutely appalled by the thought that we would now have to travel for another six hours, and we didn't know why.

No one answered me. There was nothing to say. And there was absolutely nothing to be done. The driver turned the car round and set off along the road the man in the hi-vis jacket had indicated; the road that would take us another *six* hours to reach Kathmandu, *because we were tourists*.

I don't manage very well if I'm tired, or if I'm hungry, and the constant loud music in the car began to irritate me. The drivers only had *one* CD, a compilation, and after fifteen hours we had heard it fifty times or more. I now know every word of several of Snow Patrol's numbers, and that classic, Hotel California. I am confident that I could repeat them all in my sleep, hanging upside down. And the various Indian and Nepali pieces all sounded to us like Miss Piggy on helium, on a good day, as they came round again and again.

Tod avoided a potentially nasty international incident by asking the driver to turn the music down. He obliged.

We knew we were going to be *very* late arriving in Kathmandu, so we asked the driver to phone our hotel, to tell them that we were on the way. The hotel reception staff promised to wait up for us!

We drove on and on through the darkness, and just when it seemed we had taken a wrong turning and driven into some other country, or even some other universe, the driver stopped the car and said in a very tired voice,

"We're here. This is Kathmandu!"

Wearily we got out of the car and looked around. Was he joking? It was pitch black. There was nothing to be seen beyond the portion of road we had stopped on, no light of any kind showing anywhere.

Ahh. Of course. There is no electricity in Kathmandu overnight, and little in fact during the day. It was 2am, so here we were in a power less capital city, which is something that few of us westerners have ever experienced. It was indeed a weird moment. It was not only completely dark, but it was also very quiet,

"You know Kathmandu, so which way do we go?" the driver asked us,

"Ahh, well," we said, "Not sure."

Yes, we knew Kathmandu, but not *this* part. We had never come into the city from the south east before. And anyway, it was pitch black! We could not see a thing, could not make out any landmarks, and apart from the fact that we seemed to be on reasonably high land, we had no idea where we were.

It was worryingly quiet. The four of us stood and looked around, hoping to catch sight of something, *anything* in the dark that might give us a clue, and point us in the right direction.

Suddenly I heard a sound; a strange, unfamiliar sound, reminiscent of the soft swishing of silk cloth, mingled with the gentle tapping of rubber heels on a solid wooden floor. It was coming from behind us. We all turned and squinted into the darkness. What on earth was coming?

The group of water buffalo emerged from the darkness within feet of us, and barely gave us a second glance as they separated into two groups and moved round us. There were twelve, maybe fifteen of the wonderful creatures, walking together in complete silence. A man was walking alongside the last buffalo to pass. He had one hand resting on its back, and they were walking stride for stride together. In the blink of an eye they had gone, calmly intent on reaching their destination. The group vanished into the darkness so quickly that I was left wondering if I had really seen them.

Where were they going at two o'clock in the morning in Kathmandu?

We decided to drive further into the city in the hope that Tod might recognise some landmark along the way, and started to get back into the car. In doing so we almost missed the scooter that drove past, but our driver spotted it, and ran off down the road after it shouting,

"Hello! Hello! Stop please!"

Given the circumstances I think the scooter driver was quite brave to stop. I'm not sure *I* would have done! He could well have been forgiven if he had simply ridden away from his unknown pursuer, who was dashing after him in the dark! But stop he did; luckily for us. Because not only did he **know** our hotel, but he was actually, at that very moment, on his way to an address within a whisker of it. Wow! Bit of luck!

We followed him through the dark streets of Kathmandu, which gradually became more and more familiar, even in the dark. We finally turned the corner into that short and narrow side street that we knew so well, and stopped outside the closed metal gates of our hotel.

The scooter driver began banging with his fists on the large gates, and our driver stood with his hand on the bell. Bit over the top perhaps. I hoped they weren't going to wake the whole hotel up!

But very soon the night manager and security guard opened the doors and greeted Tod and I like long lost friends.

It was good to be back. It was 2.30am.

We walked into the large and airy, dimly lit hotel lobby, and plonked down on the seats there. The manager came over and sat with us,

"You both look tired," he said, "Where have you been this time?"

We told him we had just driven nonstop from Darjeeling. He laughed,

"What! All that way? No!"

We nodded and grinned,

"Can I get you a drink before you go to bed?" he asked us, "Maybe you need one!"

"Yes! Good idea! We could murder a gin and tonic!" Tod said, laughing.

The poor man had obviously had tea or coffee, or even water in mind, but nevertheless he smiled and went off to open up the hotel bar for us.

That gin and tonic had never tasted so good!

CHAPTER EIGHTEEN

We were surprised to see our two drivers sitting downstairs in the lobby the next morning. They had intended driving straight back to Darjeeling after leaving us at the hotel, and although we thought they were mad to do so, and tried to persuade them to rest for at least a while, they had insisted on leaving straight away.

But they had discovered from the hotel security guard that there was another general strike that day in Nepal, and the guard had warned them not to drive out of Kathmandu for the next 24 hours. If they attempted to leave, he told them, they ran the very real risk of having their car seized and burned by militant strikers.

It looked as if the roadblock we had encountered, which added another six hours to our journey, probably had something to do with the general strike, although we never found out for sure.

We felt really sorry for the drivers. There was nothing for it; they would have to wait until it was safe to leave.

We wandered about the streets of the tourist area of Kathmandu, starting to say goodbye to our friends there. Our trip this time was almost finished; it was time to think about getting back to the UK.

We sat down on the steps outside one of the small bookshops, and watched the flow of tourists walking up and down the narrow street in the warm sunshine.

The bookshop was the favourite haunt of one of the few remaining street dogs in the area, and we took food to her in the evenings when we could find her.

She was small, slender and black; a quiet, gentle and loving little canine who always wagged her thanks for any food or water given to her. But she lived in the wrong country.

The previous month Nepal had celebrated the festival of Holi. It is a Hindu festival; 'the festival of colours', and has become very popular over recent years, to the extent that the streets of Kathmandu are taken over for the day by paint throwing youths, mock fighting and drenching anyone unfortunate enough to cross their paths in brightly coloured paint and powder.

One of the shopkeepers warned us to steer clear of the festivities, which we would have done anyway, but,

"There is lead in the paint," he assured us, "Be careful of it."

We had no way of knowing if that information was correct or not, but as we didn't fancy ending up like a pair of dripping kaleidoscopes anyway, we stayed indoors for the day.

That evening, when the sound of hilarity on the streets had died down, we crossed the road outside the hotel to a shop with a phone that was working.

To our surprise the little black dog was lying curled up on the shop steps. She was no longer black. She was covered in streaks of yellow and red powder. We had never seen her there before, and assumed she had sought refuge from the loud fun and games on the main street. She stood up and wagged as we dusted some of the powder off her, and she was fine. No harm done. We went into the small shop and left her sitting on the steps.

Five minutes later and Tod was speaking on the phone, when there was a loud 'crack' from outside. The shop door was open to let the cool evening air in and I turned and looked out. The little black dog was running off down the road, and a man was standing opposite the shop door with a large stone in his hand. It was obviously his second stone – he had aimed the first one at the dog, and from such close range had most probably hit her with it.

I stared at him, that ordinary, middle aged Nepali man, whose considered opinion of dogs was that they are no

156

more than vermin. He is not alone in that opinion in many parts of the world. He stared back. Between us stretched an abyss; an unbridgeable abyss.

The little black dog was there on the bookshop steps when we arrived. We gave her some food and sat down on the steps with the young man who worked in the shop. His English was good, and we had spoken to him many times before. He thought it was funny that the tourists always wanted to feed the dog,

"She should be fat!" he said. We laughed.

We didn't pay much attention when the shop's owner came out and asked the young man a question. The query was obviously about the book he was holding in his hand. We recognised it. It was 'A Beard In Nepal', our first book! We knew that the shop had several copies of it.

We sat for a little longer, and then Tod got up and went into the shop to browse. It was small, maybe 12ft by 12ft, but it was bright and welcoming, and it was crammed to the rafters with all kinds of books; not just travel books, although that section was pretty large, as you would expect in a place like Kathmandu.

A young woman, the shop's only customer, was standing by the 'Travel' shelves, flicking through 'A Beard In Nepal'. Tod went over to her and said,

"Hello. Fiona will sign that for you if you're going to buy it."

She looked up quickly, startled,

"Who are you?" she asked,

"I'm the 'Beard'" Tod said smiling, pointing to the book's title.

"Oh *sure* you are!" she laughed, "There must be *lots* of men with beards around here!"

She obviously didn't believe him! And think about it; why *should* she? Bit of a coincidence, wasn't it? You walk into a bookshop in Kathmandu, pick up a book, and hey presto the authors are right there, offering to sign it for you!

"Come and meet Fiona," Tod said, and walked to the shop door,

"Oh my God!" the young woman said, "You *are* Fiona and Tod, aren't you!"

We all laughed, and spent some time chatting with her, an American who was working in the Middle East.

You just never know who you might meet in Kathmandu!

Two days later we left Nepal again.

Nepal, that country of spectacular contrasts. From its massive, snowy mountains in the north, to its hot, flat plains in the south. From the simple, unqualified kindness of the village people who have nothing, but would give you everything, to the sometimes mercenary callousness of the town dwellers who want more.

Nepal, a country that pulls at your heart strings and fills you with elation, *and with despair*.

We love Nepal.

We are planning our next visit.

To see the photos, and to read about the other books by Fiona Roberts, please visit

http://www.spanglefish.com/fionaroberts

Printed in Great Britain
by Amazon

61872122R00089